D0982966

EX LIBRIS
PACE COLLEGE
WESTCHESTER

PLEASANTVILLE, NEW YORK

BELIEF AND UNBELIEF
SINCE 1850

H. G. WOOD

BELIEF AND UNBELIEF
SINCE 1850

CAMBRIDGE
AT THE UNIVERSITY PRESS
1955

PUBLISHED BY
THE SYNDICS OF THE CAMBRIDGE UNIVERSITY PRESS

London Office: Bentley House, N.W. 1
American Branch: New York

Agents for Canada, India, and Pakistan: Macmillan

Printed in Great Britain at the University Press, Cambridge
(Brooke Crutchley, University Printer)

BR
759.
W65

CONTENTS

CONTENTS

PREFACE

WHEN the Faculty Board of Divinity in the University of Cambridge honoured me with an invitation to deliver a second series of open lectures in the Michaelmas Term, 1953, the Chairman of the Board, Professor A. M. Ramsey, now Bishop of Durham, suggested that the course should deal 'with the movements of thought and life in the last hundred or hundred and fifty years which have shaped the present religious situation, as if to help answer the question, "How have things come to be like this as to belief and unbelief?"' Obviously, in six or seven lectures one could not hope to do more than focus attention on some outstanding features of so vast a field. I have deliberately refrained from discussing Scientific Humanism and Marxist Communism, since I dealt with them at some length in a previous course. I have only glanced at the important issues raised by the comparative study of religions, in the chapter on religious experience. I have made little or no reference to such important trends of thought as Existentialism and Neo-orthodoxy, or to such vital developments as the Ecumenical movement. But with all its inevitable limitations, I hope the book, which reproduces the lectures almost as they were delivered, will be some guide to the right understanding of the history and present position of the debatable matters handled in the chapters that follow.

I am grateful to Messrs Duckworth and Co., publishers of Lady Tweedsmuir's book *The Lilac and the Rose*, for permitting me to use the passages which appear on pp. 2 and 19 f., and to Messrs A. and C. Black for permitting me to quote at length from Dr Schweitzer's preface to the third edition of *The Quest of the Historical Jesus*, on pp. 132 and 133.

I would like to thank the Faculty Board of Divinity for giving me the opportunity of revisiting Cambridge and addressing such an indulgent audience on themes of such enduring interest.

H. G. WOOD

May 1954

CHAPTER I

1850 AND 1950: A CONTRAST

I SHALL not attempt in the chapters that follow to give a history of religious thought or even of Christian theology in Britain during the last hundred years. I have neither the time nor the ability to handle such a theme. Moreover, the book of Vernon Storr, *Development of English Theology in the Nineteenth Century up to 1860*, with its sequel, *Later Nineteenth Century English Theology*, by Dr L. E. Elliott Binns, taken along with C. C. J. Webb's masterly study of *Religious Thought in England since 1850* and the late J. K. Mozley's *Some Tendencies in British Theology, from the publication of Lux Mundi to the Present Day* makes it superfluous for me to try to do over again indifferently what has already been done so well.

What I am proposing to do is somewhat different. I shall start by throwing into relief some contrasts between the religious life and thought of Britain round about 1850 and the religious life and thought of Britain today. I shall next examine the changes in culture and in the climate of opinion which account for the contrasts. We must then consider whether we are witnessing the final dissolution of the Christian faith as some suppose, or whether the changes, social and intellectual, by which we are all affected, are leading to a more adequate understanding of the Christian faith and to a deeper appreciation of the Lordship of Jesus Christ. We shall thus be faced with the question: What does it mean to decide for Christ today?

Let us begin, then, with the contrasts. A hundred years ago, organized Christianity, including in the term both the Established Church and the Free Churches, played a greater part in the life and thought of Britain than it does today. Attendance at public worship was the normal practice of a large proportion of all classes, if not of a majority of the people. Today, if the late Seebohm Rowntree's statistics of church attendance in York may be regarded as typical of the country as a whole, not more than 10 per cent of the nation join in public worship. The adequacy of Seebohm Rowntree's data and the cogency of his inference may be questioned, but the general decline in attendance at public worship is undeniable, though its exact measure is uncertain. So far at least as the change in the practice of the members of the upper classes and of country-folk is concerned, the testimony of Lady Tweedsmuir may suffice by way of illustration.

At Moor Park [the home of the Eburys in the Victorian era], the question asked on Sundays was, 'Where will you go to church?', not 'Will you, or won't you, go?' One nearby church to Moor Park was High and the other was Low, and you attended whichever service suited your preference.

The church and its hierarchy was discussed keenly and held an important place in people's thought and conversations. Nowadays, when you stay in a house for a week-end, people often do not attend church at all, and the subject is never mentioned. Sunday is treated exactly like a week-day, even in houses where the host and hostess are people of proved integrity. The church was far more powerful in those days than it is now, and religion held a more central place in the minds of men and women.... The church-going habit I knew in my youth has completely lapsed. Men and women will go to church if they wish, but not otherwise.[1]

In this connexion, we may note that, if we have not entirely given up the idea of the Sunday as a day of rest, the old style strict Sabbatarianism which prevailed a century ago, no longer holds its ground, even in Scotland. The Lord's Day Observance Association seems to be fighting a losing battle.

If the churchgoing habit has lapsed, so also has the practice of family prayers. Probably family worship, as described, for example, in Lady Tweedsmuir's book or in H. W. Nevinson's *Changes and Chances*, has lapsed more completely than the habit of attendance at public worship. The private devotional reading of the Bible may not have been abandoned in such a wholesale manner. That there was a decline in this form of religious practice is certainly the case, but it has to some extent been arrested by the Bible Reading Fellowship and similar movements.

In the upshot, there has been a marked decline in popular knowledge both of the Bible, and of the elements of the Christian faith. H. W. Nevinson, in an article on the Bible's influence, which he contributed to the *Rationalist Annual* in 1940, lamented the fact that such knowledge of the Scriptures as formerly belonged to those who had an Evangelical upbringing, is rapidly passing away, or has indeed passed. He relates, by way of example, that the Poet Laureate, when opening the new building of the City Literary Institute in Drury Lane (14 May 1939) told how a woman had said to her friend: 'I have heard this quotation,

---

[1] Lady Tweedsmuir, *The Lilac and the Rose*, p. 85.

"Blessed are the pure in heart" and it struck me as being rather beautiful. Can you tell me where I can find it?'[1] This might be paralleled from *The House that Hitler Built*, where the author, a university professor, complimented Pastor Niemöller on his invention of the admirable slogan: 'We must obey God rather than man.' Biblical allusions in public speeches are risky nowadays. They are so seldom appreciated. Would the present House of Commons understand John Bright's allusion to the Cave of Adullam if it were made today?[2] Indeed, a distinguished French historian, in recording the incident, misinterprets it in a footnote which says, 'Allusion Biblique; Adullam a voulu tuer David.'

H. W. Nevinson sums it up thus: 'For good or evil, it is evident that such knowledge of the Bible as was our possession when I was young is fast fading away. If, when speaking from a public platform, I make some passing allusion to the Bible, I see from the blank faces of the audience that they do not understand what on earth I am talking about.' He adds that F. L. Lucas, in his journal, says much the same thing. The passage runs: 'Clearly the Old Testament is wilting in the fierce chaos of the hydro-electric age. Morality may not lose much, but I fear literature will. For the Hebrew sacred books, especially in their Jacobean English, have a grandeur missing in most modern work.'[3]

[1] H. W. Nevinson, *Visions and Memories*, p. 112.

[2] I Sam. xxii. 1, 2. 'So David escaped to the Cave of Adullam. There were also drawn together to him everyone that was in distress and everyone who was in debt and everyone who was embittered, and he became their leader.'

[3] F. L. Lucas, *Journal Under the Terror*, p. 115.

With regard to the elements of the Christian faith, the authors of the report on religion in the army during the First World War were startled to find widespread ignorance of the meaning even of Christmas and Easter, let alone other features of the Christian year. This is but symptomatic of a change in the relation of the Christian Church to the world, of which we are increasingly conscious. In preparation for the World Missionary Conference held at Tambaram in the Madras Presidency, India, at the close of 1938, Dr Kraemer wrote his remarkable study of the Christian message in a non-Christian world. Formerly we thought of Europe and the Americas as Christian, and of Asia and Africa as constituting the non-Christian world. This was the unquestioned assumption of the Victorians. But Kraemer showed clearly that 'the Christian Church, religiously speaking, in the West as well as in the East, is standing in a pagan, non-Christian world, and has again to consider the whole world as its mission-field, not in the rhetorical but in the literal sense of the word'. It is true that, as T. S. Eliot contends, in Britain we have not as a people definitely adopted an alternative creed, but we are much less positively Christian than we were; we are becoming a puzzled people. In France, it is said, 'the Catholic Church is now organizing missions to the French people on the assumption that many of them are as totally ignorant of Christianity as the heathen to whom missions used to be sent'. In England, as in other great Christian countries, there are masses of folk who have never heard of Christ within the context of religious experience. In the survey of youth in Birmingham entitled *80,000 Adolescents*, the authors invited 'the churches to

5

consider that our survey has revealed that three-quarters of the youth population of our city is completely out of touch with any form of organized religion. We are convinced that few people in the churches appreciate just how far away from them in thought and outlook these young people are' (p. 187).

The influence of organized Christianity on public life, particularly on politics, has certainly diminished. In the later nineteenth century, the Nonconformist conscience was a powerful factor in politics. It hardly counts today. One Free-Church writer says:

The Free churches are hesitant because we are banished to the wilderness and the desert, seemingly without anything to give which our contemporaries will accept; hesitant also because 'one world is dying, and the other is powerless to be born'. Yet in secular society expectancy lifts its head again. Men, though they are without God are not without hope, for they look to science and education to inspire new progress and create new liberties.[1]

Not so long ago, the Secretary of the Labour Party asserted truly and courageously that the Labour movement in this country owes more to Methodism than to Marxism. This was true in the first half of the century under survey, but can we confidently assume that Methodism or Christian Socialism outweighs the influence of Marxism in the British Labour movement today?

A hundred years ago, the Puritan tradition, with its sharp division between the Christian way of life and the life of the world, with its distrust of what we should now

---

[1] R. D. Walton, *The Gathered Community*, p. 175.

regard as innocent pleasures, with its emphasis on self-discipline and self-control, powerfully influenced all classes and all churches. If it was most influential among Evangelical Low Churchmen and Nonconformists, it was also accepted with some modifications by High Churchmen, and if it was at its strongest in the middle classes, it also affected both the aristocracy and the artisans. In Evangelical circles, the theatre, the dancing-floor and the card-table, were all suspect as worldly and dangerous to moral and spiritual welfare. Throughout the latter half of the nineteenth century, the movement for total abstinence gathered strength, particularly among Evangelicals, but in this country the ban on tobacco, which is widely observed in the U.S.A., has never been accepted, partly perhaps because some leading preachers were wedded to the pipe as inseparably as Sir Winston Churchill to the cigar. Perhaps the most remarkable of the limitations imposed by the Puritan tradition was the ban on fiction, on romances and dramatic literature. Even Shakespeare was suspect. Did not Dora Greenwell inscribe on the first page of her copy of his plays: 'All this is not of the Father, but is of the world'? H. W. Nevinson tells us, 'in my early teens I bought a Shakespeare in one volume, but my mother was so full of horror at finding it, that I hid it away. "It is a great immoral book", she said to me in one of her rare outbursts of feeling: "I know some people put it next the Bible, but that is mere wickedness."'[1] It is not surprising

[1] H. W. Nevinson, *Changes and Chances*, p. 2. Cf. W. Robertson Nicoll, *Life and Letters*, p. 37: 'The first time I ever preached in Edinburgh [in 1878] when I was little more than a boy, I introduced a quotation from Shakespeare. The minister of the Church, an exceedingly kind and

that Matthew Arnold charged Dissenters and Evangelicals with Philistinism. Such doubts about the stage, about fiction and the drama, were not the most valuable part of the Puritan tradition, but the tradition as a whole has weakened, and the very conception of worldliness is at a discount. We may have to consider later whether the anti-Puritan reaction has not gone too far, and whether we are not now in danger of overlooking the importance of 'drying the lawn somewhere', if I may recall an intriguing Spoonerism.

Allied with the Puritan interpretation of what it means to keep oneself unspotted from the world, was the idea of the world as a vale of tears, and of the Christian as a pilgrim, journeying to a better land. Bunyan was popular with the Victorians. Is *Pilgrim's Progress* still read today? Hymns about Jerusalem the Golden, in use a hundred years ago, have given place to Blake's Jerusalem, to be built in England's green and pleasant land. Instead of Watts' great hymn, 'There is a land of pure delight', we now sing J. A. Symonds' 'These things shall be: a nobler race.' The possibilities of the here and now claim attention almost to the exclusion of the hopes of another world and of life everlasting. The shift of emphasis is undeniable.

Passing from attitudes and practices to beliefs, we may note that theological doctrines were more clearly defined and better understood a hundred years ago than they are now. Common to all schools of thought was the belief in the Bible as the Word of God, and the assumption that this

friendly man, wrote to me afterwards that using Shakespeare's name in the pulpit had given great offence, and he counselled me never to do it again but to make quotations without naming the author.'

must mean that the Scriptures are free from error and discrepancy. As the record of the revelation of God's will and purpose for mankind, the Bible was treated as a manual of theology—a theology which could be presented in a defensible, rational and harmonious system. The claim of orthodox Calvinism to be the essential Biblical theology was accepted almost without reserve, in Scotland and among many Dissenters, such as the Particular Baptists.[1] The main features of Calvinism were familiar to all, though this feature or that was being called in question. The absolute sovereignty of God and the total depravity of man were among the fundamentals of Calvin's theology. Predestination meant that, by an eternal decree, God, in his inscrutable wisdom, elected some to salvation and reprobated others to eternal torment. The elect were not chosen for their virtues or their merit. They were justified by faith alone, i.e. by recognizing that they deserved eternal punishment like the rest of Adam's apostate race, and that they were pardoned because God's Son had borne the punishment of their sins in their stead. The plan of salvation turned on Christ's vicarious sacrifice. The substitutionary view of the Atonement, involving the penal satisfaction of God's justice, was held to be the correct understanding of the Cross. And this Atonement was effective only for the elect. In the 1850's this outline of the plan of salvation was regarded in many quarters as the truth of the gospel. Of course, even among strict Calvinists, the Calvinism of the seventeenth century had undergone some modification. Probably no Calvinist in 1850 believed any longer in

[1] The General Baptists were and are Arminian: the Particular Baptists were Calvinist until the close of the Victorian era.

witchcraft or in applying the sentence 'Thou shalt not suffer a witch to live' to those unfortunates who were still suspected of trafficking with Satan. But the influence of the Arminianism of John and Charles Wesley had shaken the hold of Calvinism among Evangelicals. The Calvinist view of election and reprobation was consciously repudiated by the Wesleyan Methodists. Human depravity and the need of a new birth in a sudden conversion, the pains of hell and eternal punishment, the substitutionary view of the Atonement—all these elements of Biblical theology as interpreted by Calvin, the Evangelicals retained and fervently believed. But what Charles Wesley called 'the hateful, horrible decree' they rejected. They had no doubt that Christ died for all, not just for the elect, and they held that the offer of salvation through faith in Christ and his atoning sacrifice was made to all. The hymns for the people called Methodists are variations on the theme of Christ's *all*-atoning and *all*-redeeming love. Verses 1 and 2, 5 and 6, of Hymn No. 2 may suffice by way of illustration:

> Come, sinners, to the gospel feast:
> Let every soul be Jesu's guest:
> Ye need not *one* be left behind,
> For God hath bidden *all* mankind.
>
> Sent by my Lord, on you I call:
> The invitation is to *all*:
> Come all the world; Come, sinner, thou:
> All things in Christ are ready now....
>
> Ye vagrant souls, on you I call:
> (O that my voice could reach you *all*!)
> *Ye all* may now be justified:
> *Ye all* may live, for Christ hath died.

My message as from God receive:
Ye all may come to Christ, and live:
O let his love your hearts constrain,
Nor suffer him to die in vain.

If the Wesleys repudiated the doctrines of Arbitrary Election and Reprobation, Coleridge had ventured to question the sentence of eternal torment and 'the necessity of the Abasement, Agony and ignominious Death of a most holy and meritorious Person to appease the wrath of God'. The Calvinists and the Evangelicals clung to both tenets which were increasingly felt to be repugnant to the moral sense of ordinary folk and to Christian conceptions of the love and justice of God. The questions of eternal punishment and the nature of the Atonement were, as we shall see, the issues most canvassed by serious religious thinkers in the first quarter of the century under review. In 1850 most Christians still held the traditional views of both themes. The Evangelicals played the leading role at that time, both among Churchmen and Dissenters. Individual Evangelical Churchmen, like Wilberforce and Shaftesbury, had been or were in the van in promoting great humanitarian causes. The influence of Charles Simeon pervaded the Church of England and had been consolidated by the formation of the Trust which secured and secures a considerable share in Church patronage for the Evangelical school of thought. The modern missionary movement, the child of the first Evangelical revival, was developing in a manner that was to make the nineteenth century the most remarkable era in the expansion of Christianity. The British and Foreign Bible Society in 1850 was within a year or two of celebrating its first jubilee. The Evangelical Alliance which linked Churchmen and Dissenters in a common fellowship had been founded in the 1840's. This was a defensive alliance, inspired mainly by fear of the progress of the Catholic revival. Nevertheless, it witnessed to the strength of the Evangelical revival of the 1850's.

By 1850, though Evangelicalism was still dominant, the Oxford movement had established itself within the Church of England, and the adhesion of its first leader, John Henry Newman, to the Roman Catholic Church, had given a great impetus to the Catholic revival. Theologically, the Catholics, if I may use the term loosely to cover both the Anglo-Catholics and the Catholics who accept the authority of the Pope, agreed with the Evangelicals in softening or repudiating the harsher features of popular Calvinism. Catholic and Evangelical were also at one in their view of the Scriptures as the Word of God. Indeed, at the close of the nineteenth century, Leo XIII in the well-known encyclical, *Providentissimus Deus*, was to give us the most explicit definition of the view of Inspiration as incompatible with error. The most devout Evangelical, believing in the Bible from cover to cover, could not wish for any clearer or more authoritative exposition of his faith in the verbal inspiration and inerrancy of the Scriptures. But in 1850, High Church and Low Church, Catholic and Evangelical, were hardly aware of their common ground. They were acutely conscious of their differences.

The Oxford movement did not, however, originate as a reaction against the Evangelical movement. It took its rise from fears and apprehensions aroused by changes in the character of the State, by the advance of political radicalism and of intellectual liberalism which questioned the claims of revelation and authority in religion. Ever since the repudiation of papal authority by Henry VIII, Crown and Parliament had exercised a control over the established Church which weakened its authority and independence. So long as this control was exercised by members of the Church of England, it was tolerable, but Catholic Emancipation and the removal of civic disabilities from the Jews altered the character of Parliament. The Reform Act of 1832 strengthened the Dissenting interest in the House of Commons, and was expected to initiate an extension of the franchise which would end in universal suffrage. Disestablishment, or alternatively, loose schemes of comprehension loomed upon the horizon and threatened to disintegrate the doctrinal standards and liturgical tradition of the Church.

Cambridge Evangelicals might be indifferent to the intervention of the State in Church affairs, and might regard the suppression or amalgamation of Irish bishoprics as financial common sense. Oxford theologians, still influenced by the older High Church tradition, were more alive to the dangers involved in the changing character of the State, and saw nothing less than national apostasy in this high-handed alteration in the constitution of the Church in Ireland. By what authority does the State act thus, and ought the Church to recognize it? By what authority is the Church to maintain her position, to order her affairs and proclaim her gospel? Her ministers can no longer depend on the support of the State or on the social prestige conferred by establishment. Perhaps they ought never to have depended on such support and prestige. And how is the Church to meet the questioning and sceptical secularism of the present day? The authority of Scripture is not enough. What is needed is a living personal authority to interpret the Scriptures. Otherwise we shall be lost in the chaos of private judgement. The authority which the Church must claim and assert is the authority which Christ entrusted to his Apostles when he said to them in the upper room as he stood among them in his risen power: 'Receive ye the Holy Ghost. Whosoever sins ye remit, they are remitted: whosoever sins ye retain, they are retained.' Christ thus conferred on the Apostles the right to give authoritative decisions in both faith and morals. The Holy Spirit would give them a right judgement in all things. Undoubtedly, Christ intended this authority to continue in and with the Church. It can only be exercised by a ministry which stands in the Apostolic succession, and thus derives its authority from the first Apostles. So the first of the *Tracts for the Times* invited the clergy to consider their ministerial commission. By what authority do the clergy preach the word and administer the sacrament? 'We have neglected the real ground on which our authority is built—our apostolic descent.'

Keble and Newman and their followers thus set a high value on historic continuity. The Anglo-Catholic, like the Roman Catholic and the Greek Orthodox theologians, associated tradition closely with Scripture. The developing church tradition in faith, morals and worship, must surely have been inspired and guided by the same spirit which gave forth the Scripture. The Catholic will not isolate the Scriptures as the Evangelical does. The Scriptures are to be interpreted through the Fathers. The Oxford movement up to 1850 revived interest in Patristics: it did little or nothing for Biblical scholarship. The movement also revived interest in the Anglo-Catholic divines of the seventeenth century. Newman and his associates thus recovered for the Church of England a wealth of devotional and theological literature which the Evangelicals neglected.

If the Anglo-Catholics deplored the neglect of great traditions by the Evangelicals, they also distrusted their individualism, their insistence on sudden conversions, their lack of reticence in speaking of the mysteries of the faith, particularly in preaching the Cross. Their reaction from the typical Evangelical presentation of the faith is well characterized in a paragraph in Sir James Stephen's essay on *The 'Evangelical' Succession*:

And then in obedience to the general law of human affairs, arrived the day of reaction. A new race of students had grown up at Oxford. They were men of unsullied and even severe virtue; animated by a devotion which, if not fervent, was at least genuine and grave; conversant with classical literature, and not without pretensions, more or less considerable, to an acquaintance with Christian antiquity. As they passed thoughtfully along those tall avenues, to which, a hunded years before, Whitfield and the Wesleys had been accustomed to retire for meditation, they recoiled, with a mixture of aversion and contempt, from the image of crowded assemblages and the dramatic exercises, in which the successors of those great men in the Church of England were performing so conspicuous a part. They revolved, not without indignation, the intellectual barrenness with which the Church had been stricken, from the time when her most popular teachers had not merely been satisfied to tread the narrow circle of the 'Evangelical' theology, but had exulted in that bondage as indicating their possession of a purer light than had visited the other ministers of the Gospel. They invoked, with an occasional sigh, but not without many a bitter smile, the reappearance amongst us of a piety more profound and masculine, more meek and contemplative. They believed that such a change in the religious character of their age and country was a divine command, and that a commission had been given them to carry it into effect.[1]

Perhaps I may add a word on the significance of Isaac Williams' tract *On Reserve in communicating religious knowledge*. The revulsion from or polemic against popular evangelism is apparent even in the summary of the argument of Tract 80. 'All instruments of God that benefit mankind bear the mark of reserve, which is opposite to the system of moderns, who are all for religious show and parade: the treasures of religion should be held in reserve and hid under the veil of sacred modesty: holy reserve is the authorized method of preaching the gospel, and a want of it is a breach of the third commandment, though unfortunately it is a characteristic of the present time.' In other tracts, the Evangelicals' concentration of attention on the doctrine of the Atonement was criticized and condemned. 'In the mystery of Atonement we see but the skirts of God's glory: it is not the sole pivot on which the gospel should be made to turn: the subject should not be too frequently nor too prominently brought forward: the naked exposure of it is unscriptural and dangerous: it is only one truth among many and does not absorb all:

[1] *Essays in Ecclesiastical Biography*, 5th ed. p. 447.

explicit belief in it is not absolutely necessary and the sole inculcation of it (as absolutely necessary) is subversive of all religion.' There is much more to this effect in the *Tracts for the Times*. Precisely because the sacrifice of Christ is a mystery, it is better presented in the sacrament of the Lord's Supper than in popular and sometimes vulgar preaching of a particular doctrine of the Atonement. So the Tractarians argued, and, in doing so, they brought relief to many devout souls who could not accept Evangelical theology and who were repelled by emotional evangelism. It was natural that, round about 1850, Anglo-Catholics and Evangelicals felt themselves to be poles apart.

Catholic emancipation and the conversion of many Anglicans to the Roman obedience led to a marked Catholic revival which roused the suspicions and fears of Protestants. Catholics were now encouraged to take a greater part of the public life. The old Catholic families had tended to live rather retired lives, not entering much into society or politics. Now, as it were, they came out of their protective shell. The Pope recognized the changed position and hopeful prospects of Catholicism in England by a reorganization of dioceses and provinces. The general public were startled and alarmed by this evidence of Catholic progress, and the Ecclesiastical Titles Bill of 1851 was designed to check what was called 'Papal aggression'. It was a futile panic measure of which more sober Protestants were ashamed.

It is difficult for us today to realize the strength of the feelings with which men regarded doctrinal differences in 1850. Our more easy-going tolerance may not be altogether to our credit. The Victorians took their religious beliefs seriously. Those who embraced the outlook of intellectual liberalism and would not accept the limitations Newman wished to impose on reason, took their resultant agnosticism seriously. To John Stuart Mill, Comtist and Utilitarian, the description, 'a man of unsullied and even severe virtue' could be applied as legitimately as to John Henry Newman. In the main, the early Victorian humanists and agnostics adhered to Christian, not to say Puritan, standards of character and conduct. Indeed, the unbelievers often put the believers to shame, and this experience may be reflected in the familiar lines in Tennyson,

> There lives more faith in honest doubt,
> Believe me, than in half the creeds.

In the sphere of defined belief, the lines were sharply drawn. Evangelical, Catholic and humanist or free-thinker, were acutely aware of their differences, and often found social intercourse difficult. Members of the same family would find themselves estranged from one another, and limited in the range of their common interests. Lady Tweedsmuir presents a picture of a Victorian household in her mother's time, 1880–1900, which was probably typical of many. The father, the first Lord Ebury, was a convinced Low Churchman. The mother and two unmarried daughters were enthusiastic Anglo-Catholics. The eldest son was a rather conventional Anglican. The third son, Lady Tweedsmuir's father, was agnostic, as were two younger sons, one of whom, however, married a Catholic wife. The religious situation which Lady Tweedsmuir's mother found in the home when she married the third son, she described thus:

Living in a large and heterogeneous community necessitates many unwritten laws against which, being young and inexperienced, I must often blunderingly have transgressed. One of the most important of these was the avoidance of certain topics, more especially at mealtimes or other gatherings of the whole family. Of these topics probably the most dangerous was religion, on which subject the family was sharply divided into three camps. My father-in-law was very Low Church, had in past times strongly advocated the revision of the Prayer Book, and now supported very Low Church societies and their activities. My mother-in-law and sisters-in-law were all very High Church. Unknown to 'His Lordship' they stole out to early Communion, when possible attended weekday services, took in High Church periodicals, and even concealed crucifixes in remote corners of their bedrooms. All the younger male members of the family except the eldest (who went to church but mocked impartially at High and Low Church practices) were open free-thinkers. Later on, when the younger brother married, his wife, being a Roman Catholic, brought in another variety of religious belief, but I think it was almost entirely the High Church members in the party who made the discussion of any subject even remotely connected with religion, unsafe. His Lordship would have been willing enough to live and let live, contenting himself with mildly chaffing his wife and daughters about their ritualistic tendencies. Even the regrettable opinions of his sons, though they troubled him occasionally, had never caused him to lie awake at night, or otherwise ruffled the calm of his existence. He contented himself with praying for them in the course of family prayers, read by him in the big hall, among the strange setting of heathen gods and goddesses, on Sunday evenings as well as on every weekday morning. These extempore prayers, interpolated always when the subject of them was present, and kneeling with his elbows on one of the red leather chairs in a peculiarly defenceless position, were I am sure a great satisfaction to his Lordship, who, under the cloak of a petition to the Deity, could thus safely admonish his recalcitrant children.[1]

Here, then, are represented three main strands in the religious thought of England in the Victorian era—Evangelical, Catholic and humanist. How have they been modified? What influences have been brought to bear on them, and how have their representatives responded?

[1] Lady Tweedsmuir, *The Lilac and the Rose*, p. 125.

CHAPTER II

FACTORS MAKING FOR CHANGE

THE most conservative among us cannot shut his eyes to the fact of change. Our understanding of the Christian faith has changed from the interpretation which appealed to our forefathers a hundred years ago. The world to which the faith must be presented has changed even more obviously and more radically. The climate of opinion in the second Elizabethan age is very different from the climate of opinion which prevailed in the Victorian age.

We have to recognize not only the fact of change, but also the necessity or inevitability of change. We may not sympathize with the sentiment attributed to Monsignor Ronald Knox at an early stage in his spiritual Aeneid when he is supposed to have said, 'I must have a religion and it must be different from father's', but he was right in so far as a son cannot just continue to repeat his father's phrases, or live on a merely traditional inheritance. However passionately we assert our devotion to the faith of our fathers living still, or declare that the old-time religion is good enough for us, we utter our common convictions with a different emphasis, and they sound differently in a changing world. Though there is a sense in which the Church must be *semper eadem* if she is to continue to be a Church at all, yet in many ways the claim to be always the same will prove illusory, and even as an ideal it may be misleading. A Church that never changes will fail to discharge her function as ambassador for Christ amid the chances and changes of human existence.

The movement initiated by George Fox in the seventeenth century was proudly described by William Penn as 'Primitive Christianity revived'. It was but one among many such ventures of faith, which were characteristic of the era of the Renaissance when 'Greece rose from the grave with the New Testament in her hand'. The contrast between the Christianity of the New Testament and the Christianity of the later Middle Ages leapt to the eye, and endeavours to recapture the first fine careless rapture of the primitive church were natural and vitalizing. All such ventures have their value as they recall Christians to test their doctrines, their moral standards, their institutions, by the essentials of the life and faith of the primitive Christian community of New Testament times. But simply to revive Christianity is never possible and would never be enough. There are growth and change within the pages of the New Testament itself, and we cannot legitimately halt the process of development. The Spirit of Truth, which we believe guided the formation of the Gospel traditions from Mark to John and the similar development of the different types of Christian thought which we might distinguish as Petrine, Pauline and Johannine, forbids us to try to stereotype the features of first-century Christianity. Whatever we think of Newman's tests of the true development of Christian doctrine, and however we regard the conclusion he drew from his essay, he was certainly right in affirming that, like any other philosophy or faith, Christianity would suffer change and be inevitably involved in a process of development. He said something like the last word on this issue when he wrote:

It is indeed sometimes said that the stream is clearest near the spring. Whatever use may fairly be made of this image, it does not apply to the history of a philosophy or a sect, which, on the contrary, is more equable and purer and stronger when its bed has become deep and broad and full. It necessarily rises out of an existing state of things and for a time savours of the soil. Its vital element needs disengaging from what is foreign and temporary, and is employed in efforts after freedom, more vigorous and hopeful as its years increase. Its beginnings are no measure of its capabilities nor of its scope. . . . In time it enters upon strange territory; points of controversy alter its bearing; parties rise and fall about it; dangers and hopes appear in new relations, and old principles reappear under new forms; *it changes with them in order to remain the same*. In a higher world it is otherwise; but *here below to live is to change, and to be perfect is to have changed often*.[1]

If, then, we recognize this necessity of change, we may go on to note that there will be factors making for change within and without the normal functioning of the Christian consciousness. Just because, as again Newman saw clearly, Christianity cannot be reduced to a single truth or idea, but is a complex of many elements, and just because the ideas or essentials of the Christian faith require time for their comprehension and assimilation, different groups of Christians and different generations of Christians will concentrate attention on different elements of the faith or on different aspects of the same essential elements. In the course of time, and in the light of experience, the understanding of a

---

[1] *An Essay on the Development of Christian Doctrine*, pp. 38–9.

given doctrine may be clarified or deepened, or the importance of some neglected truth may be forcibly realized. Truths which absorb attention in one generation are thrown into the shade, and other truths are made luminous and fill the centre of the stage. Examples of such shifts of interest and emphasis may be seen in the diversion of attention from the doctrine of the Atonement to the doctrine of the Incarnation, and from the Sovereignty to the Fatherhood of God, or in the movement 'Back to Jesus' which was also a movement away from St Paul. For Tolstoi as for Edwin Hatch, the Sermon on the Mount became the centre of interest to the neglect, if not to the conscious depreciation, of the letter to the Romans. We shall have occasion to note some of these changes in interest and emphasis which arose primarily from the reflection of Christian believers on the content of their faith in the light of their experience.

If we may then draw a distinction between changes in the Christian consciousness which come primarily from within, from attempting to assimilate and comprehend more fully the high and wonderful truths of Christianity, and changes which come from without, from the necessity of coming to terms with changes in secular culture and of meeting the challenge of outward circumstance and event, we shall have to consider in the second place the reaction of Christian thinkers to what have been called 'the acids of modernity'. It is the task of the theologian to wed Christianity and culture, a task that is always necessary and never finished, never easy and always dangerous. We live in a world whose culture and living conditions are dominated by natural science. Our social order, national and international, is being radically and rapidly changed by the practical achievements of science. Our views of the universe are being changed by the discoveries of science no less rapidly and no less radically. The methods of natural science are being applied, hopefully if sometimes uncritically, to our proper studies, the understanding of human nature. Along with economics and psychology, anthropology and sociology call for an assessment from the standpoint of Christian faith, an assessment which is by no means easy. The shrinking of the world and the contacts with the ancient cultures of India and China, compel a re-estimate of the relation of Christianity to the living religions of the world. Then we have to face the challenge to faith of two world wars and of violent social revolution.

How these factors, within and without, interact may be difficult to determine. Perhaps the external factors, changes in secular culture, do more than we often realize to stimulate and promote changes within the Christian mind. One of the essays of R. H. Hutton, editor of the *Spectator* in the 1870's, is devoted to the theme of 'the debts of theology to secular movements'. The debts ought to be acknowledged. A quotation may serve to illustrate the nature of such debts.

Theology has been compelled by the movement in favour of 'Toleration' to set a much higher value on that perfect spiritual freedom which is a condition of all real allegiance to God and so to elevate the cry for 'Toleration' into the demand for setting 'the heart' at liberty; the democratic movement has compelled theology to reconsider the foundations of religious equality, and discover that Christ requires the rich and great to live for the sake of the poor multitude and indeed to use their riches and power only as ministers to those who have neither riches nor power; the economic movement has compelled theology to recognize that there is a far higher spiritual service to be done by making men truly independent, i.e. masters of themselves, than by so helping them in their physical difficulties as to encourage them to lean on the generosity of others; the conceptions of justice caused by a deeper understanding of human law have compelled theology to abandon its substitutionary theory of atonement: and, finally, the scientific movement has compelled theology to abandon its conception of God as showing Himself solely or chiefly in rare and strange occurrences like miracles, and to retreat on the one great declaration of St Paul's faith in 'one God and Father of all, who is above all and through all and in all'.[1]

This thesis cannot be accepted without qualification, if it leaves the impression that the initiative lies always with the secular movements and that the advance of Christian theology is always a tardy response to a stimulus from the non-Christian world. This is far from being true. The appreciation of the spiritual freedom which is a condition of all true allegiance to God began in the seventeenth century with Baptists and Quakers, Dutch Arminians and Cambridge Platonists, John Milton and Jeremy Taylor, long before eighteenth-century rationalism lent its support to the movement for toleration. It is foolish and ungrateful to deny or belittle the contribution made by the protagonists of the Enlightenment like Voltaire and Diderot, but they were not first in the field. Nor should we overlook the contribution of the shrewd common sense which perceived that the persecution of the Huguenots was bad for trade and industry—a minor factor in the

[1] R. H. Hutton, *Aspects of Religious and Scientific Thought*, pp. 31-2.

advance of toleration which seems to the Marxists the only factor of importance and proof positive that toleration is merely a bourgeois prejudice. Undoubtedly the movement for toleration resting on secular culture forced theologians to think more seriously about the claims of religious liberty, and made them ashamed of the want of charity that has often marked the *odium theologicum*. Now, however, it is secular culture in the guise of aggressive dogmatic atheism which threatens to destroy toleration, and the challenge leads Catholic philosophers and theologians like Jacques Maritain and Father Victor White to define more exactly and defend more strenuously the demand for setting the heart at liberty.

It would, I think, be easy to prove that some of the other movements listed owe more to Christian conviction than Christian theology owes to them. This is particularly true of the democratic movement. It is of distinctly Christian origin, inspired by the fact that Jesus loved the poor and chose to be identified with them. As Horace Bushnell puts it: 'Christ, if we call him a philosopher... was the poor man's philosopher, the first and only one that has appeared.' 'His expectation is in the poor.'[1] This is the leaven of true democracy. Apart from the Christian conviction, democracy is bound to fail. Modern secular democratic movements, which sacrifice liberty and brotherhood to equality, do indeed issue a challenge to theologians to think out the nature and implications of religious equality, but, as in the case of toleration, it will be the Christian reaction to secular democracy that will save democracy, if it is to be saved at all.

[1] See Bushnell, *Nature and the Supernatural*, pp. 211 and 362.

Perhaps the clearest example of the influence of secular culture on theology is the scientific movement. That movement, too, owes a debt to Christian theism, which is generally forgotten and seldom acknowledged. But certainly the scientific movement has led theologians to pass over miracle and emphasize the wisdom and power of God in the regularities of nature, to dwell on continuity rather than discontinuity in natural process and spiritual growth, to affirm the immanence rather than the transcendence of God. Of this I may have more to say when we consider the impact of science in more detail. Now I want to pursue a little further changes in thought where the inspiration seems to me to come from reflection on the truth of Christianity in the light of Christian experience, rather than from the challenge of secular culture.

The doctrines which were most earnestly discussed in the 1850's were the belief in eternal punishment and the belief in the substitutionary penal view of the Atonement. No doubt changed views among lawyers and social reformers as to the nature and function of punishment played a part in the reconsideration of both doctrines, but the growing realization that both doctrines are incompatible with any intelligible conception of the Fatherhood of God was the more important factor in reshaping theology.

In November 1849, an undergraduate in his fourth year at Trinity wrote to F. D. Maurice, asking for guidance towards 'a satisfactory solution of a question which has long been tormenting me and which seems now to be felt universally to be of very great moment indeed...I mean the question whether any man will be hereafter punished with never-ending torments, spiritual or physical'.[1] The inquirer, F. J. A. Hort, sets out his perplexities with the exactness and judicious thoughtfulness which characterized all his later work. He is in revolt against the currently received teaching about eternal punishment, but he cannot lightly surrender a belief that seems to have such clear warrant in the Gospels and the Apocalypse, to say nothing of the Liturgy and the Athanasian Creed. Moreover, we see men becoming more hardened in impenitence every year of their lives, and if there is a further state of probation, there is no more reason why they should repent then than there was when they were on earth. And,

as we believe heaven to be the fullest communion with God in His most immediate presence.... none but those who have been separated from their sin can possibly enter into its joys. For others there would seem to be only two alternatives—an eternal curse and annihilation. I have never been able to see the alleged inconsistency in this latter notion—surely what God has originated, God can destroy, be it spirit or matter: Yet I cannot get rid of a feeling that men never are annihilated.[2]

Hort then notes how often the Epistles hint at a universal salvation which seems to exclude the idea of everlasting torments. There is force also in the Universalist objection that finite sins do not deserve an infinite punishment. In the philosophy and practice of Law, the idea of retributive justice is being rejected in favour of the ideas that punishment should be reformative and not deterrent. Can Christians retain the idea of retributive justice either in regard to

[1] A. F. Hort, *Life and Letters of Fenton J. A. Hort*, vol. i, p. 116.
[2] *Ibid.* p. 117.

future punishment or in regard to the substitutionary view of the Atonement?

The disbelief in the existence of retributive justice . . . now so widespread through nearly all classes of people . . . causes even men whose theology teaches them to look upon God as a vindictive lawless aristocrat, to stigmatize as cruel and heathenish the belief that criminal law is bound to contemplate in punishment other ends besides the improvement of the offender himself and the deterring of others.[1]

Maurice, in his reply, indicated that he had been brought up a Universalist, but had outgrown it. It was too easy-going a solution and took too little account of the weight of sin. But he was coming to the conclusion that the word αἰώνιος, translated 'eternal' or 'everlasting' in the Gospels, did not mean endless temporal succession. 'Eternal' and 'temporal' must be distinguished. Eternal life is life of a particular quality and character, not unending earthly existence. Eternal punishment, whatever else it means, cannot be never-ending torments. Eternal life is to know the love of God: not to know it is death. For the rest, Maurice refused to dogmatize. For thus throwing a cloudiness about the meaning of the word 'eternal' and for suggesting a possibility of mercy for the wicked hereafter, Maurice lost his chair at King's College, London, in 1853, but he helped his young correspondent who, at the time of his dismissal wrote: 'I fully and unwaveringly agree with Maurice in the three cardinal points of the controversy: (1) that eternity is independent of duration; (2) that the power of repentance is not limited to this life; (3) that it is not revealed whether or not all will ultimately repent.'[2]

[1] Hort, *op. cit.* p. 118.   [2] *Ibid.* p. 275.

Many years after, helping an undergraduate in 1886, in a manner similar to that in which Maurice had helped him, Hort wrote that he accepted the condemnation of the Roman doctrine of Purgatory contained in Article XXII of the Thirty-Nine Articles. He nevertheless thought

the idea of purgation, of cleansing as by fire, [to be] inseparable from what the Bible teaches us of the Divine chastisements; and though little is directly said respecting the future state, it seems incredible that the Divine chastisements should in this respect change their character when this visible life is ended. Neither now nor hereafter is there reason to suppose that they act mechanically or by an irresistible natural process irrespective of human will and acceptance. But I do not believe that God's purposes of love can ever cease towards us at any stage of our existence, or that they can accomplish themselves by our purification and perfection without painful processes. It has been well said that the heaviest sentence which could be pronounced on a sinful man would be, 'Let him alone'.[1]

A similar view had been advanced by Dean Farrar in a book, *Eternal Hope*, in 1877. He offered a rather different and less satisfactory interpretation of the word 'eternal', but otherwise he was in line with Maurice and Hort.

As an undergraduate, Hort had observed that the punishment of the hardened sinner might take the form of annihilation. Though he shrank from affirming it, it is not inconsistent with our conception of the will and power of God. 'Surely what God has originated, God can destroy, be it spirit or matter.' A little later, Edward White took up this idea. He claimed, with some justification, that this doctrine is not only consistent with our conception of

[1] *Life and Letters of F. J. A. Hort*, vol. II, p. 336.

God's sovereignty, but is actually asserted in the saying in the Gospel, 'Fear not them that kill the body but cannot kill the soul, but rather fear him who can destroy both soul and body in Gehenna.' The natural immortality of the soul is a Platonic rather than a Biblical doctrine. Conditional immortality appealed as true to many prominent Christian thinkers in the latter part of the nineteenth century, including Agar Beet among the Methodists, and R. W. Dale among the Congregationalists. The episode of the button-maker in Ibsen's *Peer Gynt* embodies the same conception. Gehenna itself suggests the burning up of rubbish rather than the endless torment of immortal souls. Of course, there were many among both Catholics and Evangelicals who protested their belief in the traditional concepts of hell-fire—Newman and Pusey among Catholics, Spurgeon among Evangelicals. But this confession lost its edge till we come to a recent orthodox definition to the effect that we must believe in hell-fire but need not believe that any-one will go there. As the century wore on, the doctrine of hell-fire figured less and less in preaching. Preachers no longer shook sinners over the mouth of hell. Dale could say in 1874: 'The doctrine of our forefathers has been silently relegated, with or without very serious considera-tion, to that province of the intellect which is the house of beliefs which we have not rejected, but which we are willing to forget.'[1]

The letters that passed between Hort and Maurice are the best introduction to the reconsideration of the doctrine of eternal punishment by devout and Christian thinkers two generations ago. The emotional conflict in the minds

[1] A. W. W. Dale, *Life of R. W. Dale*, p. 312.

of more simple believers was admirably interpreted by
George Macdonald in some of his novels. The epitaph on
David Elginbrod's father touches the theme somewhat
lightly.

> Here lie I, Martin Elginbrod,
> Have mercy on my soul, O God!
> As I would do, if I were God
> And you were Martin Elginbrod.

It voices the growing conviction that a God who con-
demns sinners to hell for eternity would be less merciful
than sinful men and women. More serious is the picture of
Robert Falconer's grandmother, wrestling in prayer for
the soul of his father—her son, Andrew, presumed to be
lost. I translate the Scots of the passage.

Gladly would I look upon his dead face if I could believe that
his soul was not amongst the lost. But oh! the torments of that
place and the smoke that goes up for ever and ever, smothering
the stars. And my Andrew down in the heart of it, crying! And
me not able to get to him. O Lord, I cannot say, Thy will be
done. But don't lay it to my charge: for if you were a mother
yourself, you would not put him there (for gin ye war a mither
yersel, ye wadna pit him there).

But the whole scene where Robert Falconer listens to his
grandmother expostulating with God, needs to be read, to
realize the anguish of the whole situation.

Where do we stand now? We have given up the literal
understanding, or misunderstanding, of the imagery in
which future punishment was depicted. Probably no one
now believes in an eternity of physical torment for un-
repentant evildoers. In a famous case before the Judicial

Committee of the Privy Council, a judgement was described as dismissing hell with costs! At least from that time on, no member of the Church of England was required to believe literally in the flames of hell. Hell-fire no longer figures in popular preaching. Some would say that we hear too little about future punishment and the danger of being lost eternally. Both the motives for missionary work abroad and the sanctions for morality among ourselves, it is often supposed, have been weakened by the surrender of the belief in hell. An interesting comment by an old man of eighty is cited by Rowntree and Lavers in the chapter, 'How honest is Britain?' in their book, *English Life and Leisure*. He said:

I believe that unless people are restrained by some active religious belief, or are disciplined by fear, they will always be dishonest. When I was a boy we were taught to be afraid of hell —When I became a man I decided that the religious training I had received was not true and I became an agnostic. But even then I wished with all my heart that the religious teaching was true, because I foresaw that as more and more people ceased to believe it, every sort of crime and wickedness would grow. Looking back over eighty years, I have no hesitation in saying I have watched a steady growth of dishonesty—and it is still growing.

The old man went on to specify new factors. The fear of consequences has declined. Prison is not so terrible a thought as it used to be. There is greater temptation to be dishonest today, and the incessant need of money puts a premium on fraud. The effect of two wars is obviously detrimental to quiet honest citizenship. Rowntree and

Lavers add: 'We believe that our elderly friend's diagnosis is a true one, and, like him, we place the principal emphasis on the decline of religious belief.'[1]

The old man's anticipation of the disastrous consequences that would follow when men were no longer restrained by the fear of hell was endorsed by more conservative theologians such as Newman and Pusey, Dr Jelf and Canon Liddon, and was one of the factors, but only one, which inspired the tenacity with which they held on to the old doctrine. But, as Dr Dale saw, you cannot retain or revive a doctrine you no longer effectively believe because it once inspired missionary zeal or restrained evil-doers. To hold a religious belief to be true because, if true, it bolsters up morality, is to have religion on false pretences, as Dr Martineau rightly insisted.

In my judgement, the best survey of all the main issues involved in the nineteenth-century discussions is J. H. Leckie's *The World to Come and Final Destiny* which was published in 1918. He analyses the threefold outcome of the great argument which began in all seriousness with the dismissal of Maurice from King's College in 1853. In the upshot, you had Christian thinkers of distinction committing themselves to a belief either in eternal punishment or in conditional immortality or in universal salvation. Dr Leckie pointed out that each of these beliefs has some firm support in the Scriptures, and each is vitally related to some aspect of the Gospel. The first emphasizes the seriousness of our moral decisions. Individuals and communities are called upon to face issues on which their welfare here and hereafter depends. For good or ill, the

[1] *Op. cit.* p. 227.

decisions men make are momentous. The consequences of sin and wrongdoing continue in all their wretchedness unless transformed by repentance and forgiveness. Nor will conversion be forced. God waits to be gracious and men may for ever refuse to return to him. There are days of opportunity and visitation, and we suffer loss, perhaps eternal loss, if we neglect our opportunities and miss our day of visitation. As I have already suggested, belief in conditional immortality reminds us not only that the Greek conception of the natural immortality of the soul is not a Biblical doctrine, but also that immortality is God's gift—God's gift in Christ, and that death, the disintegration of human personality, is the natural outcome of sin. But if we think of the wonder and power of the love of God to us in Christ, we cannot but embrace the hope that, as Origen argued, all at last shall be subject to Christ, and subject to him as all true believers long and delight to be subject to him. The Good Shepherd seeks the lost sheep until he finds it. Will he ever give up or accept failure? The same parable insists on the shepherd's desire to possess his complete flock. He is not content to lose even one. And does not Christ inspire in us the same longing to see mankind complete in him?

> The wish that of the living whole
> No life may fail beyond the grave,
> Derives it not from what we have
> The likest-God within the soul?
>
> (*In Memoriam*, LV)[1]

[1] Cf. the remarkable saying of Charles Péguy: 'What will God say to us, if some of us go to him without the others?'

Perhaps today Tennyson and Dean Farrar voice the feelings of most Christians.[1]

The other theme which much exercised the minds of Christian thinkers in the third quarter of the nineteenth century, was the traditional doctrine of the Atonement. The view still generally accepted in 1850 was, that to satisfy God's justice and to make forgiveness possible, Christ bore the punishment of our sins by surrendering his body to death on the Cross. This substitutionary view of the Atonement undoubtedly brought relief to many consciences burdened with the sense of guilt. The experience of Charles Simeon in 1779, recalled by Mr Pollock as the prelude to his history of the Cambridge Inter-Collegiate Christian Union, was repeated in succeeding generations, and in 1850 was regarded as the normal form of conversion. Charles Simeon, preparing for communion by reading either *The Whole Duty of Man*, or William Law's *Serious Call* felt that he could never make himself a worthy communicant. A passage on the meaning of the Old Testament sacrifices, in a book by Bishop Thomas Wilson, came to his deliverance. 'What!' thought Simeon, 'May I transfer my guilt to another? Has God provided an offering for me that I may lay my sins on another? Then I will not bear them a moment longer.' And then and there as he wrote: 'I sought to lay my sins on the sacred head of Jesus.'[2] The substitutionary view of the Atonement not only freed men from the burden of their sins, but also filled them with love for the Christ who gave himself for them. Moreover,

[1] See also J. A. T. Robinson, *In the End, God*, and John Baillie, *And the Life Everlasting*.
[2] J. E. Pollock, *A Cambridge Movement*, p. 3.

the doctrine lent itself to simple statement in effective preaching. On the other hand, it raised disquieting issues in morality and theology. Why should penal satisfaction of God's justice be necessary to enable God to forgive sin? Is there any virtue in forgiveness if the full penalty for the offence to be forgiven has been paid or borne by a third innocent party? Does human forgiveness proceed on any such principle? Is the satisfaction of God's justice anywhere insisted on as the prerequisite of forgiveness in the sayings or parables of Jesus? Parables like the story of the two debtors, or of the Prodigal Son, do not suggest that God's anger must be appeased and his justice satisfied before he freely forgives. Moreover, the popular view seemed to set the justice and mercy of God in opposition to one another, and even to contrast God the Father with God the Son, the first person of the Trinity corresponding almost to Marcion's just God of the Old Testament, and the second person of the Trinity representing Marcion's good God of the New. The purpose of Christ's death would then seem to be to reconcile God's justice with God's mercy, and this involves a failure to understand both justice and mercy and the relation between them. The substitutionary view of the Atonement represents Christ as a kind of third party mediating between God and man, and this hardly does justice to the great truth 'God was in Christ reconciling the world to himself'.

The difficulties of the traditional view and the sense of the need for a re-interpretation are well expressed in the same letter of Hort to Maurice in which he raised the question of eternal punishment. He writes:

Then there is the question of Substituted Punishment, which, as it seems to me, is quite distinct from the Atonement and reconciliation of the person of sinning man and God. I can at most times thankfully contemplate the fact of God's forgiveness (in the strict sense of the word: that is, the removal of estrangement from the offender, irrespective of the non-enforcement of penalties) and His delight in humanity as restored through its Head: but surely this has little to do with the principle that every offence must receive its just recompense. The father may forgive the child and yet cannot justly exempt him from the punishment of disobedience. 'Amen!' says the evangelical: 'the penalty must be paid somehow by somebody. The penalty is tortures to all eternity for each man. Christ, in virtue of the infinity which he derived from His Godhead, was able on earth to suffer tortures more than equivalent to the sum of the eternal tortures to be suffered by all mankind: God must have the tortures to satisfy His justice, but was not particular as to who was to suffer them,—was quite willing to accept Christ's sufferings in lieu of mankind's sufferings.'

O that Coleridge, while showing how the notion of a fictitious substituted righteousness, of a transferable stock of good actions, obscured the truth of man's restoration in the Man who perfectly acted out the idea of man, had expounded the truth (for such, I am sure there must be) that underlies the corresponding heresy (as it appears to me) of a fictitious substituted *penalty*![1]

Hort's summary brings out the insuperable difficulties of the traditional doctrine as popularly conceived and as often preached, but he still feels that there is truth underlying it which needs to be restated. Outstanding among many who tried to do what Coleridge had failed to do, were

[1] *Life and Letters of F. J. A. Hort*, vol. i, pp. 119–20.

J. McLeod Campbell and R. C. Moberly. McLeod Campbell, who had been deprived of his charge by the General
Assembly of the Church of Scotland for asserting with
Coleridge and the Wesleys that Christ died for all, not
simply the elect, proceeded to work out his ideas in a book
on *The Nature of the Atonement* which appeared in 1856.
The Atonement presupposes the Incarnation, but the
Incarnation is incomplete without the Atonement. Christ
witnesses for the Father to man, and he represents humanity
to God, and if he is to represent humanity to God, he
must be completely identified with his brethren, he must
share the burden of their mortality and the consequences
of their sin. His death on the Cross thus completes the
Incarnation. But the work of Christ is to be understood as creating the true personal relations between
God and man. To interpret the death of Christ in terms
drawn from the law and law courts is to misconceive it.
The sufferings of Christ are not the measure of what God
can inflict as the punishment of sin, but the revelation of
what God feels with regard both to sin and sinners. The
Fatherhood, rather than the Sovereignty of God as empha-
sized by Calvin, is the central interest of this approach to
the Atonement. A similar approach is to be found in the
sermons of F. W. Robertson of Brighton and in the
writings of F. D. Maurice.

McLeod Campbell's work, or rather the parallel interpretation of the death of Christ in the writings of the
American theologian, Horace Bushnell, did not satisfy
Dr Dale. He recognized how inadequate the traditional
legal terms were in which the doctrine of the Atonement
had been expressed. We must move in the realm of personal

relations, not in the realm of legal obligations. But if the death of Christ is a revelation of what God feels about sin, it must reveal the resentment of perfect righteousness in God's reaction against sin, and so Dale, in his great work on the Atonement (1875) found a place for asserting that Christ bore the punishment of sin. Robertson Nicoll re-affirmed Dale's position in a book, *The Return to the Cross* (1897), which drew this appreciation from Handley C. G. Moule, who was at the time Principal of Ridley Hall:

Very specially, I have again and again given thanks for your strong and reasoned witness to exactly that range of truth—the truth of guilt and of Cross-won remission and acceptance—the *nulla propter Christum condemnatio*—which is now so widely ignored if not rejected—and the absence of which seems always to me to bring a long and dreary falsetto into the whole music of theology.[1]

It was R. C. Moberly, in his *Personality and Atonement* (1901), who carried further some of McLeod Campbell's insights, declaring that Dale was still one-sided in his emphasis on the notion of penal suffering, and that the Atonement was still being treated without due reference to the work of the Holy Spirit and the life of the Church. But I cannot do more than note Moberly's original conception of Christ as the perfect Penitent, the One who expressed the full reality of penitence.

I would like to add a few reflections on this discussion of the doctrine of the Atonement in the nineteenth century. I think that the movement of thought represented by McLeod Campbell and R. C. Moberly was necessary and

[1] William Robertson Nicoll, *Life and Letters*, p. 160.

healthy, and yet it has not given us the exposition of the truth underlying the traditional indefensible doctrine which Hort desired. Few will question that Evangelical theology isolated the Atonement in a dangerous manner, as if Christ's death were all that mattered. It seems to me that Schlatter's judgement was right. 'Jesus had no occasion to attach to his death any special object beyond that served by his whole activity. He died in order to be able to do in eternal perfection what He was always doing: namely, to call men to repent, to forgive, to set men free, by making visible the majesty of God's mercy.' We might add, 'by making visible the cost of God's forgiveness'.

Then our present reading of the New Testament suggests that the earlier interpretation of the Atonement misunderstood or underestimated some vital elements in New Testament teaching. Two or three instances may be noted. It was no accident that, in describing the ministry of reconciliation in II Cor. v, St Paul says that God in Christ was reconciling the world to himself. Christ died to reconcile men to God, not to reconcile God to men. Christ died not to change God's attitude to men but to change men's relation to God, to deliver men from a predominantly legal relation to God as ruler and taskmaster, and to bring them into a true personal relation to God as Father. In some important passages, where the Authorized Version uses the word 'propitiation', the Revised Standard Version prefers the word 'expiation'. The first word suggests something done to appease an angry deity, the second is concerned with cleansing the guilty conscience. McLeod Campbell observed rightly that in the Old Testament, sacrificial offerings are connected with worship rather than with law, with cleansing from the pollution rather than with deliverance from the punishment of sin. Undoubtedly, the writer to the Hebrews understands the death of Christ in this way. The idea of appeasing God's anger had no place in the New Testament. The anger of God, as St Paul conceived it in the opening of Romans, is a process of intellectual and moral disintegration which is the consequence of sin. Christ died to save us from the wrath of God by reversing this process. The time is ripe for a reformulation of the nature of the Atonement in the light of our present-day scholarship.

The truth behind the heresy of a fictitious substituted penalty is that Christ in dying has done something for us which we could never do for ourselves, has done all that is needed to reconcile us to God. We may never be able to state this in terms which satisfy us intellectually, though we shall still be able to sing, and sing sincerely, 'Rock of Ages, cleft for me, Let me hide myself in Thee'. Here, I find Marcel's distinction between a problem and a mystery helpful. A problem is a puzzle for which you may hope to find a solution, a question to which you may give a rational answer. A mystery is a fact of experience which you cannot hope to fathom or understand, with which and by which you have to live. It is a mistake to treat problems as mysteries and close down the search for rational solutions before you are obliged, and there are problems connected with the theme of Atonement which we may still try to unravel. But it is a mistake to treat mysteries as problems, and at long last the Atonement is not a problem but a mystery, a depth where all our thoughts are drowned.

CHAPTER III

THE IMPACT OF
NATURAL SCIENCE

OBVIOUSLY a short chapter on the influence of
natural science on religious thought in this
country over the last hundred years cannot be
more than a personal estimate of some main features of the
story. It is impossible to avoid the use of the big brush,
though one will try to avoid the *slovenly* use of that utensil
which Lord Acton so rightly deplored in history.

We have witnessed in the last hundred years the growing
prestige of natural science. The recognition accorded to
science in Cambridge at the beginning of the period was
very modest. The Natural Science Tripos had been insti-
tuted and the examination held for the first time in 1851.
It is interesting to recall that F. J. A. Hort took the
examination and was placed second in the list of those who
were awarded First Class Honours, R. D. Liveing
heading the list. Hort examined in the Tripos in Botany in
1855 and again in 1872, the year in which he delivered his
Hulsean lectures. Is there another example of an examiner
in the Natural Science Tripos being Hulsean lecturer in the
same year? If the recognition of natural science was
modest, at least it commanded the interest of some of the
best minds who came through the test of the old double
first in classics and mathematics. Though the Tripos was
inaugurated in 1851, the provision of scholarships and
fellowships for natural science did not develop on any

large scale until the abolition of religious tests in the older universities in 1871. This act was revolutionary in a double sense. The admission of Dissenters to the university changed the relations of Church and Dissent, made possible the Student Christian Movement, which in turn has promoted and fostered the Ecumenical movement. The better understanding between Anglicans and Free Churchmen has brought about the more recent developments in national education, particularly the recognition of the place of religious instruction based on agreed syllabuses. It is difficult to exaggerate the importance of the difference in the religious life and thought of this country which has followed from the fruitful association of Church and Dissent through the abolition of religious tests. But perhaps the impetus given to the study of the natural sciences was even more important. The proper recognition of natural science was at length secured in Oxford and Cambridge. In the redbrick universities which started in Birmingham and Manchester in the last quarter of the nineteenth century, the Faculty of Science was the dominant partner from the start. Throughout our century, the prestige and influence of natural science have grown steadily, until today our culture is, in the main, the reflection of scientific humanism. Here, undoubtedly, is the primary factor in creating the change of outlook outlined in the first chapter. The prestige of natural science and the concentration of so much of our attention and interest on natural science, has led to a decline of interest in religion in general, and in Christianity in particular. A writer in the weekly journal, the *Inquirer*, recently characterized the change in a way that seems to me true in the main:

Probably the revolution that has had the profoundest effect upon religion in modern times is not that caused by science itself, but by the absorption of the scientist in his science. He feels no need to go outside its range for intellectual and emotional satisfaction. Religion to him is not so much a closed book, as one that need not be touched at all. This, of course, is not true of all scientists, but it is probably true of most. Consequently, some of the most influential and active minds of the day are cut off entirely from religious reflexion. They set up for themselves and other people a climate of opinion in which religion need play no part. This was not always so. Science, in its infancy, even only a few centuries ago, offered little attraction to active minds. There was not enough of it. Men had to go to philosophy, or theology, or religion, or all three combined to find full satisfaction. That is not so today. On the face of it, intelligent men can completely ignore religion and everything connected with it and at the same time lead, apparently, full and satisfactory lives.

The advance of applied science is no less important and influences the outlook of the ordinary man even more profoundly. The marvels and conveniences of modern technics—the cinema, the radio, television, the motor-car and the aeroplane—all tempt us to live on the surface of life and to avoid contact with ultimate reality. The very pace at which we live and work today strengthens this tendency. We can fill up our time with innocent recreations, mostly provided for us, and we thus surrender to what H. G. Wells called 'everydayishness'. The popular Sunday Press knows its business. It provides sensations and eschews problems. Play on people's emotions; do not ask them to think. It is easy to exaggerate this tendency, but of its existence and strength there can be no doubt. In the early days of the Revolution in Russia, Trotski confidently expected the cinema to replace the church. He was over-confident, but it was a shrewd anticipation.

Bertrand Russell has drawn attention to another aspect of the advance in technics.

> Science as technique has conferred a sense of power: man is much less at the mercy of his environment than he was in former times. But the power conferred by technique is social, not individual: an average individual wrecked on a desert island would have achieved more in the seventeenth century than he could now. Scientific technique requires the co-opera-tion of a large number of individuals organized under a single direction. Its tendency, therefore, is against anarchism and against individualism, since it demands a well-knit social structure. Unlike religion, it is ethically neutral: it assures men that they can perform wonders but does not tell them what wonders to perform. In this way it is incomplete....The philosophies that have been inspired by scientific technique are power-philosophies—ends are no longer considered: only the skilfulness of the process involved.[1]

I suppose the natural scientist may be described as sedu-lously paying court to Madame How and becoming as sceptical about the existence of Lady Why as Betsy Prig was about the existence of Sairey Gamp's friend, Mrs Harris. The general effects are, first, a concentration on the development of our technics without much thought about the ends to be served by the means at our disposal, and, second, the assumption that in the realm of ends we are our own masters and shall soon be able to refashion the world nearer to our heart's desire.

[1] Cf. *History of Western Philosophy*, pp. 755 f. and pp. 855–6.

It has long been apparent that scientific habits of thought may and do make the approach to religious truth difficult for many. The very idea of dogma as religious thinkers often present it is repugnant to the scientific attitude. For the scientist all theories are tentative and provisional, and the theologian often claims a certainty, an irreversibility for dogma which is unacceptable to scientists who have found even Newton subject to revision by Einstein. The idea of relativity is supposed, quite mistakenly, to favour relativism in the realms of truth. There are no final truths in natural science, and we must be content with fragmentary and even seemingly inconsistent findings instead of the constructions which please the systematic theologian. Moreover, the scientist insists on the constant appeal to experience, on exact measurement and observation, and he is prepared to suspend judgement where evidence is vague and scanty, and where the test of a crucial experiment is not available. Where his methods of investigation cannot be hopefully applied, he doubts whether knowledge is possible.

> We have but faith; we cannot know,
> For knowledge is of things we see.

The questions, then, that science cannot answer, we must not waste time in asking. So Freud concludes: 'Science is no illusion. But it would be an illusion to suppose that we could get anywhere else what it cannot give us.'[1] The only reality, or at least the only reality accessible to us, is the reality disclosed by the evidence of our senses, our sense-perception being aided, extended and tested by all the

---

[1] S. Freud, *Future of an Illusion, ad fin.*

instruments and techniques at the disposal of the modern scientist. Many present-day positivists 'confess frankly that the human intellect is unable to find conclusive answers to many questions of profound importance to mankind, but they refuse to believe that there is some "higher" way of knowing, by which we can discover truths hidden from science and the intellect.'[1]

Indeed, some exponents of logical analysis go further, and declare that the questions that science cannot answer must be meaningless. The simple, not to say naïve identification of all genuine knowledge with natural science raises a barrier to the recognition of any truth in religion.

It may also be legitimate to recall Charles Darwin's confession that his devotion to science killed his interest in poetry and music. His was not an isolated case. It was a mathematician who read Milton's *Paradise Lost* and asked what it proved, expecting apparently the lucidity and cogency of a geometrical demonstration in the poet's handling of his great argument. And it must have been a scientific-sociologist who stumbled over two lines in Tennyson's *Vision of Sin*,

> Every moment dies a man,
> Every moment one is born,

and criticized the poet on the ground that he should have written 'Every moment one and one-fifth is born'!

Before the end of this chapter, I must examine a little more in detail the claim to omnicompetency made for science and the associated refusal to recognize the true

[1] Bertrand Russell, *History of Western Philosophy*, p. 864.

boundaries of science. But before I pursue that theme further, I must say something about the impact on religious belief and thought of the findings of some particular sciences.

Before our century begins, the advance of geology had led men to question the accuracy of Archbishop Ussher's dating of the Creation in the year 4004 B.C. As the date had at one time appeared in the margin of the Authorized Version, it was sometimes regarded as Holy Writ, and in any case, the date seemed to be the natural conclusion from Scriptural evidence. But it was the publication of Darwin's *Origin of Species* in 1859 which created a more serious upheaval in orthodox circles, and indeed required a re-thinking of many traditional views. Few Christians were as ready to welcome the new theory of evolution as F. J. A. Hort, who wrote to Westcott in March 1860: 'Have you read Darwin? How I should like a talk with you about it! In spite of difficulties, I am inclined to think it is un-answerable. In any case, it is a treat to read such a book.'[1] More representative, at least of the reaction of the rank-and-file members of the Churches were the two old ladies who said: 'Let's hope it's not true, and if it is, let's hush it up!' For anyone who perceived the significance of Darwin's work, it was no longer possible to regard the accounts of creation in Genesis as scientific and historical narratives. That the opening chapters of Genesis are myths had now to be frankly recognized. It was little to the credit of Christian people that they had taken so long to reach this understanding of the nature of these records of beginnings. As far back as 1497, Dean Colet, living not only before

[1] *Life and Letters of F. J. A. Hort*, vol. I, p. 414.

Darwin and Newton, but also before Copernicus, realized that the first chapter of Genesis should be regarded as 'a poetic fiction', a popular presentation of the story of creation with no claim to be science or history. Colet could see this because, as a Platonist, he could see that a poetic fiction might convey essential truths. The Church in general failed to follow him because the value of the myth as a vehicle of truth had been forgotten.

Moreover, in the course of the discussion of Darwin's *Origin of Species*, evolution was freely contrasted with creation, as if an insight into the method or process of creation entitled us to dispense with the very idea of creation, and enabled us to explain the existence of the Universe without assuming the existence of a creator![1] Conservatives clung to the literal sense of Genesis because they feared a surrender would endanger the truth of creation. They had some excuse. Far too much was being claimed for evolution. It was some time before we discovered that, as P. T. Forsyth put it, evolution is a good servant, but a bad master! In the once popular poem of which each verse ended with the refrain, 'Some call it evolution; others call it God', it seemed as if one name was as good as the other. Evolution was put forward not just as a convenient descriptive label for a highly complex process, but as a cause that accounted for everything. But the criticism which Sidgwick passed on evolutionary sociologists had its application to biologists: 'They (the Sociologists) mistake

---

[1] By a similar perversity, J. B. Bury treated Providence and Progress as mutually exclusive ideas. He failed to find a natural law of progress, but if he had found it, it would not have made the idea of Divine Providence less credible.

the statement of a problem for its solution and delude themselves into the belief that they know the laws of evolution of society because they have a clear conception of the general fact of social evolution.'[1] The early impression that natural selection and the struggle for existence would account for everything in a quasi-mechanical fashion was an illusion. Darwinism was supposed to eliminate all traces of purpose or design by explaining evolution as the necessary result of the struggle for existence. But let us admit that there is destruction of some and survival of others in a mechanical or quasi-mechanical fashion in virtue of their nature: that explains nothing at all. It is merely asserting that things are at each moment what they are and not otherwise. The survival of the fittest sounded impressive until the Marquis of Salisbury pointed out that it means simply, the survivors do survive.[2]

The more serious challenge of Darwin lay, not in offering the evolutionary process as a substitute for God, but in re-directing attention to those aspects of nature which are difficult to reconcile with the wisdom and love of God. Tennyson's lines about nature 'red in tooth and claw' were not based on Darwin's account of the struggle for existence. *In Memoriam* appeared nine years before *The Origin of Species*. But Darwin's work underlined the great difficulty of Theism. Both the tentative and negative characteristics of the process of biological evolution as Darwin conceived it were a trial of faith.

'Men ask how an omniscient mind which knows precisely what is wanted can set Nature groping her way for-

[1] *Henry Sidgwick, A Memoir*, p. 421.
[2] See additional note on p. 61.

ward as if she were blind, to find the path of least resistance. And again, they ask how, if bad only becomes good by steady starvation of the worse, it is possible to see in this process the cherishing love of a divine Creator?'[1] It is not surprising that in this country many tried to find in the Life-Force or in evolving world-stuff or in cosmic process, a substitute for God, and while claiming to reverence and serve the Life-Force, regarded it as a blind, blundering force which only arrives at consciousness in men. It seemed inappropriate to conceive the Life-Force in terms of Fatherhood, and indeed if we identify God with the Life-Force, we can hardly speak of him as the God and Father of the Lord Jesus. But, as we shall see, no religion or philosophy of the Life-Force is really defensible.

The influence of Darwinism on men's thoughts on social process and social progress differed according as men concentrated attention on the struggle for existence, or on the accumulation of small variations which it was supposed led to the emergence of new species. Marx, thinking first of the struggle, found in class-war and violent revolution the clue to history and the source of progress. The accumulation of small variations is only significant when a growth in quantity issues in a change in quality. The Fabians, on the other hand, regarded evolution as the opposite to revolution. Gradual change, at times almost imperceptible, was the mode of true progress. Alfred Marshall put in the title-page of his *Principles of Economics* the motto 'Natura non facit saltum'. Once, after attending a lecture on Mendelism, I asked Marshall whether it was true that nature never makes a jump. He replied, 'Only very little

[1] R. H. Hutton, *Aspects of Religious and Scientific Thought*, p. 48.

ones'. This was pure original Darwinism, which stands in need of Abbé Mendel's qualifying discoveries. The emphasis on the struggle for existence required the modification to be found in Kropotkin's *Mutual Aid* and Henry Drummond's *Ascent of Man*. And today, Julian Huxley points out that all war, including class-war, so far from finding support in biological evolution, is condemned as suicidal by the discovery that 'on the biological level intraspecific competition is often not merely useless but harmful to the species as a whole'.[1]

Another disturbing aspect of Darwinism was the demonstration of the kinship of men with the lower brute creation. This was a challenge to human pride rather than to Christian faith, though Samuel Wilberforce's unfortunate sally at the meeting of the British Association in Oxford was based on the assumption that a religious interest was at stake. The supposition, however, that here was a serious conflict between Darwinism and Genesis rests on a misunderstanding. The best commentary on the verses in Gen. i which refer to the creation of man in God's image is, to my mind, Dr Julian Huxley's essay, 'The Unique Status of Man'. It is a false humility which belittles or denies the profound differences between the consciousness of human beings and the consciousness of animals. We are distinguished from the rest of the animal world by our capacity to form and entertain general ideas and to apply them freely to circumstances and situations other than those in which they were formed. Alike as a praying animal and as a cooking animal, *homo sapiens* differs from the most intelligent of his humbler kinsfolk. The passage at arms

[1] Julian Huxley, *Evolutionary Ethics*, pp. 45–6.

between Bishop Wilberforce and T. H. Huxley was really a storm in a tea-cup, a quarrel over an essentially subsidiary issue.

Indeed, the whole Darwinian controversy may now be regarded as an affair of outposts. In theology, the idea of evolution favoured the acceptance of the idea of progressive revelation. This in itself paved the way for an understanding of the Scriptures which would assert their essential unity without placing all the writings on the same level of inspiration, and without attaching to them the same kind of authority. It was possible to justify the refusal of the early Church to separate the Old Testament from the New without endorsing that reverence for the letter of the Old Testament which has often distorted Christian thinking. Apropos of Marcion's difficulty in harmonizing the just God of the Old Testament with the good God of the New, Rendel Harris used to say: 'In theology it is a mistake to be born before Darwin.' In many ways Darwin has contributed to an enrichment of Christian thought. But other advances in natural science have offered more serious challenges to faith.

The mysterious Universe revealed by modern astrophysics renders obsolete the theology of the Leather Bottèl. It is no longer possible to believe that this vast Universe has been brought into existence simply for the use and benefit of man. When we consider the heavens today, we do not wonder with the Psalmist at the fact that the God who made heaven and earth cares for man: we tend to doubt the fact. We hesitate to address the strange, inscrutable power behind the Universe as Father. If, with Sir James Jeans, we suppose this power to be a mathematician, such a God might claim the worship of a select few in Cambridge; he could hardly be the object of devotion for mankind. Lowes Dickinson fell back on IT rather than HE. 'The last word lies with what I am in the habit to myself of calling IT. IT is probably up to something, though perhaps to nothing that interests us ephemerals.'[1]

In passing, I may note that, if the developments of modern astrophysics make it difficult for many to believe in the Fatherhood of God, they also reveal the weakness of the religion of the Life-Force. So far as our scientific knowledge goes, the activity and the career of the Life-Force are severely limited in both space and time. It belongs to this little wayside planet, takes its rise here and will perish on the day the earth becomes uninhabitable. As Bertrand Russell says somewhere, the religion of the Life-Force is parochial, not universal, and, as Dr Inge pointed out in *God and the Astronomers*, it is the worship of a mortal God.

The sciences of biology, physiology and psychology combine to throw doubt on the hope of personal immortality. We men are psycho-physical organisms, and the association of mind and body is so intimate that it is difficult to conceive the existence of mind or soul apart from body. Gilbert Ryle is busy laying the ghost of the conception of mind as an independent existence. The advances in our knowledge of the working of the brain bid fair to reveal all the secrets of human consciousness. Moreover, the general idea of biological evolution still favours the idea that the individual is significant only as a link between

[1] *Memoir*, p. 228.

generations. To hand on the lamp of life, burning we hope a little more brightly because we have held it, should content us. We ought not to ask for any other immortality.

If the general idea of evolution carries with it the conception of life as going on and on and up and up, such a conception seems to preclude us from attaching supreme value to any achievement or personality in the past. All men's past achievements are to be surpassed, are but stepping-stones to higher things. If we are swayed by this current of thought, we shall hesitate to attach any finality to the Christian gospel or to admit the Lordship of Jesus Christ. Unless I mistake, many young folk under the influence of modern science will be inclined to say, 'Jesus may be humanity's best yet, indeed we acknowledge him as a leader because we know no one better, but to go further is to commit oneself beyond the evidence. If we look for a superman, with Shaw and Nietzsche, must we not look also for a super-Christ?'

Finally, there is the challenge to any and every form of religious faith which comes from psychology, particularly from the Freudian school of psychoanalysis. In many circles it is now taken for granted that religion is an illusion, the child of wishful thinking. Possibly there is no department of science where it is at once more necessary and more difficult to determine boundaries, than it is in psychology.[1] Here we have to face the most fundamental issues.

Some of the issues raised by the impact of science will call for closer examination later. In particular, the nature of religious experience will be the subject of a later chapter.

[1] May I here recommend *The Boundaries of Science* by John Macmurray ?

But in closing the present argument, let me venture to add two or three reflexions.

First, there is nothing in the essential character and findings of natural science which should make any believer hesitate or be ashamed to say: 'I believe in God the Father Almighty, Maker of heaven and earth.' There is indeed much in modern science, particularly in astrophysics, which puts in question not our faith in God, but the adequacy of our conception of God. 'Your God is too small' is the challenge involved in many of the revelations of natural science. But what Martin Buber has called 'the eclipse of God' at the present time is due to the concentration of our interest on the understanding and control of nature. We are so preoccupied with nature as a going concern, that we forget the Creator. W. T. Stace, in his recent book, *Religion and the Modern Mind*, observes, in my judgement correctly, 'the transition from the teaching of early science to a diminishing belief in God was a psychological not a logical transition. *In other words, it is a mistake*'.[1]

Second, the essential character of natural science seems to me incompatible with any form of naturalism or materialism. The findings of particular sciences may indeed seem to merge man in nature and explode any supernatural pretensions, but science in itself favours a different estimate of human nature and destiny. Take this curiously one-sided view of the significance of great scientific discoveries from Llewellyn Powys:

The human race has suffered three great humiliations: when Copernicus showed the earth was not the centre of the

[1] W. T. Stace, *Religion and the Modern Mind*, p. 225.

universe: when Darwin proved that man's origin was not the result of a direct creation: when Freud explained that man was not the master of his own thoughts and actions. It must endure an increment of ignominy before it will be prepared to temper its demands. 'Nothing is in the intellect that was not before in the senses.' In the monstrous matrix of matter, how fallible and paltry appears the miracle of mentality.[1]

This is a strange reading of the human situation. Apart from the misunderstanding of the nature of Freud's discoveries and the failure to realize the importance of Leibniz's addition to the sentence about the intellect and the senses—'There is nothing in the intellect that was not before in the senses, nothing, that is, except the intellect itself'—the so-called humiliations due to Copernicus, Darwin and Freud, are really so many triumphs of the scientific intelligence. In the matrix of matter, mentality is indeed a miracle, and the miracle, so far from being paltry, becomes more wonderful with every advance of science. Science would not exist if man were not in some degree master of his thoughts and actions. Scientific inquiry is a spiritual activity, not possible for things or animals, only possible for rational persons. Science is itself the standing disproof of materialism, the clear evidence of the truth of Sir Thomas Browne's description of man as the great amphibium, a creature designed to live in two worlds, the physical and the spiritual, the natural and the supernatural. Two early Greek philosophers made complementary contributions to a primitive theory of knowledge. One said, 'We know by similars, by kinship'; and the other, 'We know by contrasts, by difference'. We

[1] Llewellyn Powys, *The Pathetic Fallacy*, pp. 126–7.

may combine the suggestions. We could not know nature if we were not in a real sense part of nature, and we could not know nature if we were not in a real sense above nature, different from nature. If the earth is our mother, God is our Father, and we need faith in God as our Father to save us from a mother-fixation to earth.

Thirdly and lastly, though the fundamental faith of the scientist, loyalty to truth, is always obligatory, and though the methods of inquiry characteristic of the natural science laboratory must be used to the full in every realm, including the study of human nature and human society, yet we cannot accept the view that the only genuine knowledge of nature and ourselves is to be found in the natural sciences, and that such knowledge as the natural sciences give us is the more genuine and reliable as each science approximates to the precision of physics and chemistry. Incidentally, the idea that, because all sciences in a sense depend on physics, they will all eventually be reduced to or deduced from physics, is an illusion. The idea that, given a sufficient amount of initial data, Laplace's calculator, with the basic laws of physics, could account for everything in our universe, including human history, is again a mistake. I ventured once to put it concretely thus: If he had but the time, and I had but the brain, Bertrand Russell could explain modern physics to me, but no advance in physics will ever explain Bertrand Russell to me. History is a science, but it is a science *sui generis*, not to be reduced to physics or even to anthropology and sociology. There are limitations to the knowledge to be obtained by the methods of natural science, as L. P. Jacks reminded us in his study of a psychologist among the saints, a study of a psychologist who wished to be converted in order to study the process of conversion! Some forms of knowledge that matter most to us can only be won by spiritual adventure. By all means look before you leap, but in the end, leap you must. Maritain is right. There are differing degrees and differing forms of knowledge, and not all of them come under the head of natural science.

I am always glad when I find myself in agreement with Bertrand Russell. Towards the close of *The Scientific Outlook*, he wrote:

> The desire for knowledge has another form (from that characteristic of natural science) belonging to an entirely different set of emotions. The mystic, the lover and the poet are also seekers after knowledge—not perhaps very successful seekers, but none the less worthy of respect on that account. In all forms of love, we wish to have knowledge of what is loved, not for purposes of power, but for the ecstasy of contemplation. In knowledge of God stands our eternal life, but not because knowledge of God gives us any power over Him.[1]

ADDITIONAL NOTE

Canon Raven recently drew attention in a public lecture to a remarkable passage in the presidential address to Section D, Zoology, by Dr Pantin, delivered in Edinburgh in 1951. It runs as follows:

> In the child's constructional model of a crane we discern not one principle of design but at least two. For there is the design of the set of parts so that they shall build such things as cranes as well as the special design of the crane. In the living organism

[1] Bertrand Russell, *The Scientific Outlook*, p. 270.

we can ascribe the apparent design of its immediately adaptive features to natural selection. Can we discern design in the properties of the units which make such an organism possible? These properties of the units are not the result of selection in the Darwinian sense. And if we see design in them we must say with Du Bois-Reymond '—Whoever gives only his little finger to teleology, will inevitably arrive at Paley's discarded *Natural Theology*'. Natural Selection bowed Paley and his argument from design out of the front door in 1859: and here he would come climbing in through the back window saying that he owns the title-deeds of the whole estate! Fortunately it is for the metaphysicians to examine his claims and not for me.[1]

Probably the metaphysicians will not favour a return to Paley's conception of the relation of God to the physical universe as parallel to the relation of a clock-maker to a clock. The Universe is not that kind of mechanism. But it is apparent that selection in the Darwinian sense has not disposed of the presence of design in our world. The idea that it had done so was always an illusion, born of wishful thinking.

[1] *The Advancement of Science*, vol. VIII, no. 30, p. 145.

CHAPTER IV

LITERARY AND HISTORICAL CRITICISM: THE STRENGTH AND WEAKNESS OF A HISTORIC FAITH

I F the publication in 1859 of Darwin's *Origin of Species* precipitated the discussion of issues involved in the relation of religion to science, the appearance of *Essays and Reviews* in the following year called forth an even more strenuous controversy over the application of the canons of historical inquiry and literary criticism to the interpretation of the Scriptures. That the essayists were asking for trouble is manifest, though they probably never anticipated the violence of the reaction which their essays evoked. The volume was edited by Benjamin Jowett who contributed the longest, and perhaps the most important of the essays, that on the interpretation of Scripture. His colleagues included Frederick Temple and Mark Pattison. But the prime mover was probably Dr Rowland Williams, Vice-Principal of St David's College, Lampeter, whose review of Bunsen's *Biblical Researches* was deliberately provocative. He constantly challenged orthodox theologians by disparaging estimates of their theological principles, and irritated them by estimates as disparaging of their scientific equipment. The common purpose of the writers was to secure more freedom for critical inquiry. The dominant schools of thought in the Church of England were producing an atmosphere of restraint and even insincerity. *Essays and Reviews* was an attempt to let in fresh air by breaking a window.

Hort had been invited to contribute to the book, but he declined for two reasons. While he fully sympathized with their desire to maintain absolute freedom of criticism, science and speculation, he had more sympathy with High Churchmen in their views of Church, Ministry, Sacraments and Creeds, than had the Essayists. He also felt this manifesto was unwise. He regarded the enterprise very much as Erasmus regarded Luther.

The errors and prejudices which we agree in wishing to remove can surely be more wholesomely and also more effectively reached by individual efforts of an indirect kind than by combined open assault.... As a mere matter of prudence, it seems to me questionable to set up a single broad conspicuous target for the Philistines to shoot at, unless there is some very decided advantage to be gained.[1]

Hort's anticipations were more than justified. The essayists were soon involved in a storm of ecclesiastical censure. They were violently attacked in the *Quarterly Review*. An episcopal letter condemning all the essays without much qualification or discrimination was drafted indeed by Wilberforce, but signed by most of the leading bishops, including Tait and Thirlwall. Two of the essayists, Dr Williams and Dr Wilson, were put on trial for heresy and, though they were acquitted on appeal, both Houses of Convocation passed resolutions reaffirming their condemnation of the book. When Gladstone appointed Temple to Exeter in 1869, Pusey wrote him a letter of

[1] A. F. Hort, *Life and Letters of F. J. A. Hort*, vol. i, p. 400.

protest. Though Temple refused to make any declaration before his appointment was confirmed, he subsequently withdrew his essay from publication in order to avoid giving offence to the weaker brethren. Disapproval of Benjamin Jowett and his essay on the interpretation of Scripture took a meaner form. For years the proposal of the Hebdomadal Council at Oxford to raise the annual salary of the Professor of Greek from the exiguous sum of £40 to the modest figure of £300 was thrown out by the clerical vote. Those who came to the defence of the essayists against the Philistines risked their chance of preferment. When Dean Stanley, who regarded the publication of the book as a mistake, took up the cudgels on behalf of his friends in the *Edinburgh Review*, his mother wrote to him: 'I am very glad that you have written this, not that I agree with it all, but because it puts out of the question your ever being a Bishop.' 'I was annoyed at the time,' said Stanley, 'but now I see she was right.'[1]

The ecclesiastical authorities tried to discredit the book by indiscriminate censure and heresy-hunts. Sidgwick wrote to *The Times* in February 1861, protesting that the laity required an intelligent answer, not prejudiced abuse.

We want a reply which will take each essay separately, discussing it fully and fairly, entering into the writer's point of view.... If they (the essayists) can be met and refuted on their own ground, the publication of the book will have been a blessing to the Church; for we cannot ignore the fact that the thoughts they have expressed have been floating vaguely through the minds of many. The way in which they have hitherto

[1] Prothero and Bradley, *Life and Correspondence of A. P. Stanley*. vol. II, p. 41.

been handled will increase their influence, I think, upon the mass of the English laity: it will increase their influence, I am sure, upon the youth of England.[1]

About the same time, Hort and Westcott seriously considered securing signatures for a declaration in these terms:

We, the undersigned clergymen of the Church of England, desire to protest publicly against the violent and indiscriminate agitation now being directed against a book called *Essays and Reviews* and against the authors of it. Believing that the suppression of free criticism must ultimately be injurious to the cause of truth and religion, we especially regret the adoption of a harsh and intolerant policy, which tends to deter men of thought and learning from entering the ministry of the Church and to impel generous minds into antagonism of the Christian faith.[2]

This declaration never appeared as it failed to secure adequate support. Hort's sympathies continued to be strongly on the side of the essayists, and he followed the legal proceedings against Williams and Wilson with close attention. Writing to Ellerton after the two had been condemned in the lower court, he said,

I suppose... the defendants have already appealed on the judgment itself: if so, I cannot help hoping that the superior court will think itself justified in assuming a semi-legislative power and laying down the widest toleration for the clergy as well as the laity. I am convinced that now and for some time to come, mere naked freedom of opinion is the great thing to strive for as the indispensable condition of everything else.[3]

[1] A. and A. M. Sidgwick, *Henry Sidgwick, A Memoir*, p. 65.
[2] A. F. Hort, *Life and Letters of F. J. A. Hort*, vol. i, p. 439.
[3] *Ibid.* p. 457.

In the upshot, the Privy Council reversed the first decisions in the lower court, and the final judgements declared that the clergy were not obliged by the formularies of the Church to believe and teach either the verbal inspiration of the Scriptures or the doctrine of eternal punishment, or the Calvinistic 'doctrine of imputed righteousness'. If Hort welcomed these decisions as safeguarding the liberty needed for honest critical inquiry, Dean Church perceived serious dangers in the appeal to the Privy Council to decide issues in Church doctrine. Indeed, the proceedings in the case of Dr Williams and Mr Wilson raised far-reaching issues into which we cannot now enter—such issues as 'the ethics of subscription to the Articles', the relations of Church and State, and the right limits of comprehension within the Church of England. As Dean Church put it: 'The question really calling for solution is—How to reconcile the just freedom of individual teachers in the Church with the maintenance of the right and duty of the Church to uphold the substantial meaning of her body of doctrine?'[1] He did not think the right solution could be found in the Privy Council assuming a semi-legislative power and determining the limits of toleration for the Church.

The negative, not to say the provocative, character of many of the essays, accentuated the violence of the reaction, and created the popular impression that criticism, lower and higher, is the embodiment of the spirit that denies. This was manifestly unfair to Benjamin Jowett's contribution, which may still be read with profit by all serious students of the Scriptures. It was sheer misrepresentation

[1] R. W. Church, *Occasional Papers*, vol. II, p. 46.

to suggest that his insistence on the precept 'Interpret the Scriptures like any other book', meant that Jowett regarded the Scriptures as no different from or no better than, any other book. He went out of his way to avoid any such misunderstanding of his position. Two quotations put the matter quite clearly.

No one who has a Christian feeling would place classical on a level with sacred literature.... But, however different the subject, although the interpretation of Scripture requires 'a vision and faculty divine', or at least a moral and religious interest which is not needed in the study of a Greek poet or philosopher, yet, in what may be termed the externals of interpretation, that is to say, the meaning of words, the connexion of sentences, the settlement of the text, the evidence of facts, the same rules apply to the Old and New Testaments, as to other books.[1]

In a later passage, he adds:

When interpreted like any other book, by the same rules of evidence and the same canons of criticism, the Bible will still remain unlike any other book: its beauty will be freshly seen, as of an original which is restored after many ages to its original state: it will create a new interest and make for itself a new kind of authority by the life which is in it.[2]

The real issue is, shall we understand the Scriptures, or shall we go on with traditional interpretations which ignore their true nature and obscure their original meaning?

The first duty of the scholar is to determine the original meaning of the author whose work he is studying. The older methods of interpretation, based on the assumption

[1] *Essays and Reviews* (2nd ed.), p. 337.   [2] *Ibid.* p. 375.

that the Scriptures are uniformly, verbally, and mechanically inspired, the writers being merely passive instruments
used by the Spirit of God, precluded any such approach to
the understanding of the minds and intentions of the
writers. Jowett argued that the older methods of interpretation must be abandoned if we are really to understand and
honour the Scriptures. This would apply to the mystical
allegorical method of interpretation, beloved by the Fathers
and defended by the Oxford Tractarians. It also involved
a rejection of the literalism so popular among Protestants.
To take everything literally is to confuse imagery with
statements of fact, poetry with prose. It is a refusal to
recognize the variety of literary form in the collection of
writings which constitute the Scriptures. In the Old
Testament we have myth and legend: contemporary
memoirs and later tendentious narratives: we have poetry,
proverb, prophetic oracle, and law. Not to appreciate different literary forms is to rest in a disastrous literalism. We
must also beware of the influence of rhetorical interpretation—the reading of meanings into texts for the sake of
edification and present-day applications. In the main,
Jowett's case stands, as do his canons of criticism. There is
very little in his essay which a modern scholar would wish
to retract, though he might agree with Hort that Jowett
gave to some critical observations more weight than they
deserved.

Again, Jowett rightly argues that we must not bring
some *a priori* notion of the nature of inspiration to our
interpretation of the Scriptures. 'The nature of inspiration
can only be known from the examination of Scripture.
There is no other source to which we can turn for informa-

tion: and we have no right to assume some imaginary doctrine of inspiration like the infallibility of the Roman Catholic Church.'[1] Moreover, 'any true doctrine of inspiration must conform to all well-ascertained facts of history and science'.[2] It was quite clear that the older conception of inspiration, which Christians shared with Jewish writers like Philo and Josephus, was no longer tenable. But it was very hard for Christians to surrender a point of view so deeply ingrained, which seemed indispensable for the maintenance of the authority of the Bible. Westcott was working out a conception of plenary inspiration which might obviate the more serious defects of the belief in verbal inspiration. Jowett seemed content forcibly to bring out all the difficulties of the older view, without providing a satisfying alternative, though no doubt he would have agreed with the negro ministerial candidate who was being examined by a divinity board of which the members were sharply divided on the question of inspiration, and who, when asked for his views on inspiration, replied: 'I think the Scriptures are sufficiently inspired for all practical purposes.'

The reluctance to abandon cherished beliefs was intelligible, as were also the apprehensions regarding the probable development of critical inquiries. Orthodox and rationalist were both ensnared in the all-or-nothing fallacy. Either everything in the Scriptures is inspired and true, or nothing is. The absurd negation of rationalism is the natural counterpart of mistaken claims of inerrancy and infallibility advanced by the orthodox for the Scriptures. But there were features of the early critical movement

[1] *Essays and Reviews*, p. 347.   [2] *Ibid.* p. 348.

which aroused legitimate distrust. One was the acceptance by many critics of Hume's dictum, 'Miracles do not
happen'. Even Matthew Arnold, who did so much to foster
a right appreciation of the Bible as literature, thought that
'there is nothing one would more desire for a person or
document one greatly values than to make them independent of miracles'. But no historian today would dismiss so
cavalierly, as rationalist critics did, narratives containing
features deemed to be miraculous. Another ground for
caution was a feature of critical inquiry which was more
prominent in the work of German scholars than in similar
studies in England. Speaking of three types of scientific
workers, Sir Richard Gregory includes among them 'the
iconoclast—the breaker of images—rebelling against
authority, impetuous to prove that the old ideas are false'.
So among critics, the desire to be original often issues in
seeking the sensational novelty that will shock traditional-
ists. The essayists, particularly Dr Williams, were pleading
for a proper valuation of the remarkable developments of
critical inquiry among German scholars. Some years later,
reviewing Mrs Humphry Ward's *Robert Elsmere*, Dean
Church put his finger on a certain weakness in German
scholarship which compels caution in accepting their
findings.

German learning is decidedly imposing. But after all there
are Germans and Germans; and with all that there has been of
great in German work, there has also been a large proportion of
what is bad—conceited, arrogant, shallow, childish. German
criticism has been the hunting ground of an insatiable love of
sport—may we not say, without irreverence, the scene of the
discovery of a good many mares' nests? When the question is

asked, why all this mass of criticism has made so little impression on English thought, the answer is, because of its divergencies and variations, because of its negative results. Those who have been so eager to destroy have not been so successful in construction. . . . Answers, and not merely questions, are what we want, who have to live and work and die. Criticism has pulled about the Bible without restraint or scruple. We are all of us steeped in its daring assumptions and shrewd objections. Have its leaders yet given us an account which it is reasonable to receive, clear, intelligible, self-consistent and consistent with all the facts, of what this mysterious book is?[1]

We are still waiting for the assured results of Higher Criticism, and many doubt whether the kind of account of the faith of Israel and of Christian origins which Dean Church desired will ever be given us. Earlier in the twentieth century, many of the intellectual leaders whom I admired as an undergraduate were sceptical about the possibility of a faith associated with history. Thus, Bertrand Russell at one time held that 'historically, it is quite doubtful whether Christ ever existed at all, or, if he did, we do not know anything about him'. Lowes Dickinson, in a little book *Religion, a Criticism and a Forecast*, which deservedly attracted a good deal of attention when first published, argued that to base faith on history is to build on quicksands. He wrote:

Those acquainted with the nature of historical enquiries, the uncertainty of testimony, the prejudice of witnesses, the doubtfulness of documents—who have watched, in other religions than the Christian, the growth of myth and the crea-

[1] *Occasional Papers*, vol. II, pp. 185–6.

tion of fictitious personalities, may easily assure themselves, without entering far into the laborious enquiry, that its results are bound to be in the highest degree tentative and uncertain, that scholars to the end of the chapter will continue to disagree and to dispute, and that, in fact, there is not evidence sufficient in quality or in quantity, to establish any unquestionable final truth. In an ordinary historical enquiry, this might be a matter of small moment.... But it is a very different matter when men are asked to stake their whole conception of life on the dubious result of enquiries so difficult. And a man who thinks about the issue at all, will, I believe, incline to set aside the whole controversy as irrelevant to whatever is really essential in religion, and seek elsewhere than in history, the basis on which to erect the fabric of his belief and conduct (pp. 37–8).

In a letter much later, Lowes Dickinson reaffirmed this judgement:

My difficulty about Christianity is and always has been, that Christians make the centre of their faith the historical existence of a man at a certain age. I daresay he *did* exist, though that has been doubted. But if he did, what was he really like? I cannot think that religion can depend upon such uncertainties.[1]

Lowes Dickinson had his reserves about Christian standards, but he thought historicity should not affect the appeal of such standards to those who accepted them.

A man may indeed find a religious inspiration in the recorded life and sayings of Christ. But the inspiration would be the same whether he regarded the record of the Gospels as myth or

[1] E. M. Forster, *G. Lowes Dickinson*, p. 212.

as fact, and would depend not on the existence of Christ in the past or in the present, but on the conception of life embodied in his story.[1]

Some Christian thinkers, sensible of the difficulties of a historical faith so persuasively set forth by Lowes Dickinson, sought to cover the deficiencies of historical evidence and to establish religious certainties, by an appeal to religious experience, specifically Christian or more vaguely mystical. The many issues involved in this appeal to experience will be the subject of the next chapter, but let me now give one illustration from Dr Inge's essay on the sickness of Christendom in *The End of an Age*. He wrote: 'What should be our attitude towards the 'fact-like stories' as Von Hügel calls them, which are parts of dogmatic theology? They have a spiritual meaning, but is the connection with historical fact essential?'[2] Dr Inge found essential invulnerable Christianity in the mystic's understanding of human nature: 'There is a soul-centre which can never consent to sin, a spark, as they said, kindled at the altar of God himself.'[3] So essential Christianity springs ever fresh in the hearts of men, and the Christian mystic will not be much concerned about the results of critical inquiry. Let the discussion of myth or fact in the Gospels go as it may, essential Christianity will not be affected. This is very close to Lowes Dickinson's position, but Dr Inge accepted more fully than Lowes Dickinson the conception of life embodied in Christ's story, and believed in the historical character of the record, though regarding the question of historicity as of secondary importance.

[1] G. Lowes Dickinson, *Religion, a Criticism and a Forecast*, pp. 38–9.
[2] *The End of an Age*, p. 95.   [3] *Ibid.* p. 64.

I cannot myself rest satisfied with this view of the nature and progress of historical inquiry, or dismiss our understanding of past events as non-essential or irrelevant to our religious faith. There is progress in historical study. Scholars may go on disputing and disagreeing to the end of the chapter, but they do not go on disputing and disagreeing about the same things. Lord Acton's ideal standard of exactness and impartiality which would ensure that the life of Luther would be essentially the same whether written by a Catholic or a Protestant, may never be attained, but we do arrive at closer approximations to that ideal. Because the historian deals in probabilities, and cannot in many regards get beyond probabilities, though some are such high probabilities as to be moral certainties, and other interpretations of past events so clearly more probable, that the acceptance of the less probable or merely possible view borders on intellectual dishonesty, we cannot neglect the findings of the historian because he cannot offer us the same kind of evidence as the natural scientist offers. Because the historians' judgements cannot be established by some crucial experiment, and there is always room for doubt and question, the ass among historians can retain his lion's skin longer than he can among natural scientists. But I am tempted to suggest that Lowes Dickinson's picture of the negative results of historical inquiry, particularly in the field of Christian origins, is the impression left on the minds of those who do not enter very far into the laborious inquiry. Furthermore, if we form our conception of life without regard to history, the only result will be that our conception will be wrong, or at least inadequate. 'Probability', said Bishop Butler, 'is the guide of life', and we dare not dispense with it. A saying of Richard Whately is also relevant: 'God made the moon as well as the sun: and when he does not see fit to grant us the sunlight, he means us to guide our steps as well as we can by moonlight.' If the findings of the historians are less certain, less luminous than those of the scientists, we must still guide our steps by them. There is wisdom and insight in an early judgement of Henry Sidgwick on the main issue we are considering. At the age of twenty-four, he wrote to H. G. Dakyns, who seems in 1862 to have raised something like Lowes Dickinson's doubt:

Now to your 'Can Faith depend on facts?' Why, if I had to think that a man's damnation or salvation depended on a right view of historical facts, I allow I should feel an insuperable difficulty in the thought you so express. But I do not see why the *best* development of humanity should not be conditioned thus. That is all. A man may be a very fine man as a Theist or Positivist, and may have a very valuable faith; but supposing the most powerful informing and inspiring faith is only obtainable from ideas which depend on a right view of historical events—why is this inconceivable? As a matter of fact, we see one kind of Faith is better than another—as judged by average results. Why should not the Christian faith be the best?[1]

Moreover, it is not possible to concede to Lowes Dickinson that the inspiration which a man may find in the record of the life and sayings of Christ would be the same whether he received the record as myth or as fact. That, surely, is an academic fallacy. A conception of life is more intelligible if it is presented in a story rather than in abstractions, and it

---

[1] *Henry Sidgwick, A Memoir*, p. 82.

becomes more effective if the story belongs to real life, and not to the world of imagination. Canto XXXVI of Tennyson's *In Memoriam* is still valid:

> For Wisdom dealt with mortal powers
> Where truth in closest words shall fail,
> When truth embodied in a tale
> Shall enter in at lowly doors.
>
> And so the Word had breath, and wrought
> With human hands the creed of creeds
> In loveliness of perfect deeds,
> More strong than all poetic thought.

When Bertrand Russell and Lowes Dickinson toyed with the Christ-myth theory and alternatively suggested that, even if Christ were a historic person, the gospels give us no reliable information about him, they were not representing the direction and outcome of historical inquiry into Christian origins. The Christ-myth theory is not taken seriously, except on the other side of the Iron Curtain. And when Mr Rupert Furneaux, popularizing the ingenious but unsubstantial theories of Robert Eisler, in his recent book *The Other Side of the Story*, hazards the judgement that 'in the Gospels all that which represents genuine Palestinian tradition could be written on half a sheet of paper', he only shows that he is completely out of touch with the present position of the critical study of the Gospels. What he meant and should have said is that in the Gospels the only details which can be twisted into support of Eisler's thesis could be written on half a sheet of paper.

The real challenge of critical inquiry, as it appeared to the readers of *Essays and Reviews*, lay in another direction. If the critical views of the Old Testament literature were accepted, we should have to admit limitations to the knowledge of Jesus, which seemed to most Christians, Evangelicals and Catholics alike, to be incompatible with belief in the Incarnation. The issue was raised acutely by the use of Psalm cx in the passage in Mark xii, where Jesus appeals to the Psalm as a word of David in order to prove that the Messiah must be more than son of David, must in fact be great David's greater Son. But if David did not write the Psalm, what becomes of the argument? Orthodox believers might be persuaded to recognize errors and discrepancies in the Old Testament writings, but can we admit errors in the recorded utterances of Jesus?

The seriousness of the issue can hardly be exaggerated, and the reluctance to accept the conclusions of the critics is readily intelligible. But the facts in the case compelled attention, and once some limitation of Christ's knowledge was recognized, men had either to give up their traditional belief in the Incarnation or to reinterpret it. Mrs Humphry Ward, in her novel *Robert Elsmere* chose the first alternative. Her hero abandons faith in the divinity of Christ, but tries to live by his teaching and example. He ceases to believe in Christ as Lord, but still follows him as leader. Charles Gore chose the second alternative, and in his essay in *Lux Mundi*, as well as in his Bampton lectures, interpreted the Incarnation as meaning that the Word of God took flesh at a particular time and as man accepted the limitations of the culture of his age and people. He found support for this interpretation in the letter to the Philippians, where Paul says that Christ Jesus, who existed originally in the form of God, counted it not a prize to be clutched at to be on an equality with God, but emptied himself, taking on him the form of a slave, becoming in the likeness of man. ἐκένωσεν ἑαυτόν, 'he emptied himself', he laid aside the prerogatives of Deity in order to become man. From the Greek verb was derived the word *kenosis*, the self-emptying of Christ, as necessarily involved in any true Incarnation. Reviewing the theology of *Robert Elsmere* when it appeared in 1880, R. H. Hutton grasped and stated the essential issues. He wrote:

There is a singular confusion in the mind of the hero of this book as to the need for infallibility in the human organ of divine character and teaching, the sort of infallibility which any divine revelation to man must in his opinion be supposed to involve. He seems to think that the evidence of any human error in the Gospels, or of any local or traditional limitation in the human mind of Christ is proof complete that God is not revealing himself in it. I should have thought, on the contrary, that a divine revelation through a human medium and a human nature is impossible without involving human error. . . . It is unreasonable to expect that Jesus of Nazareth should have discriminated between a prophet like Isaiah, whose prophecies belong to the time to which they are referred, and a prophet like Daniel, who is now regarded as the product of an age much later than that suggested by the author. I should as soon expect our Lord to have understood in his human intellect and have rectified in his human career, the astronomy of the age, as to have understood and corrected the scholarship and criticism of the age. But does it follow from this that the divine nature was not manifested in such a human nature in the only manner in which God *could* be manifested in the life of a given age and race and country—that is, by a perfect personal fusion between the human nature whose conditions God had assumed, and the divine nature which had assumed them? The inference would be most unreasonable.[1]

Under the guidance of Charles Gore and the *Lux Mundi* School, High Churchmen accepted the new understanding of the Incarnation more readily than the Evangelicals. Not that the decision was easy. The older leaders, Pusey and Liddon, were shocked by Gore's teaching and remained unconvinced. The younger men increasingly looked up to him as the interpreter both of the Incarnation and of the social implications of Christianity which were indeed for Gore the direct outcome of the gospel of the Incarnation. Robert Elsmere's devotion to social service was endorsed by those who thought his Unitarianism an inadequate basis for the social gospel.

In conclusion, I may recall a wise caution of Richard Hooker which should never be forgotten in our consideration of these high matters. It is a master-principle in theology that what is worthy of God must be true to him, but we are poor judges of what is worthy of God. The history of religious thought is strewn with mistaken theories based on the assumption that the authors knew what was worthy of God. Orthodox and unorthodox theologians are among the offenders. The Deists of the eighteenth century assumed that essential Christianity must be as old as creation and must be free from all mystery because it would not be worthy of God to have withheld the knowledge of the essentials of religion from the meanest intelligence from the beginning of time. Yet the actual religious history

[1] R. H. Hutton, *Contemporary Thought and Thinkers*, vol. II, pp. 267–8.

of mankind disproves the assumption. Jew and Christian alike assumed that the Scriptures, to be the word of God, must be inerrant and infallible. The conviction rests, not on the evidence, but on the assumption that only such a record would be worthy of God. But, says Hooker,

in matters which concern the actions of God, the most dutiful way on our part is to search what God hath done, and with meekness to admire that, rather than to dispute what he in congruity of reason ought to do.... When we do otherwise, surely we exceed our bounds; who and where we are, we forget: and therefore needful it is that our pride in such cases be controlled, and our disputes beaten back with those demands of the blessed Apostle, 'How unsearchable are his judgments and his ways past finding out! Who hath known the mind of the Lord, or who was his counsellor?'[1]

[1] *Laws of Ecclesiastical Polity* (Everyman ed. vol. 1, p. 358), book III *ad fin.*

CHAPTER V

RELIGIOUS EXPERIENCE

FREDERICK TEMPLE anticipated that the centre of interest in theology would shift in the nineteenth century from metaphysics to psychology. The transition was most manifest in the publication in 1902 of William James' Gifford Lectures on *The Varieties of Religious Experience*. William James did not confuse psychology with philosophy, or regard psychology as a substitute for philosophy, but his work focused attention on the psychology of religion. The very title of the Gifford Lectures was a service to the understanding of the claim and nature of religion. There is a strong tendency among Christians to stereotype religious experience. The Methodists and, later, Evangelicals, insisted not only on the necessity of conversion, but on the necessity of conversion conforming to a particular type or pattern. The Catholic insisted on the importance of particular channels of grace and found it difficult to believe that grace could be received through any other channels. The Quaker is inclined to doubt whether we can worship in spirit and in truth except on the basis of silence. It was altogether to the good that Christians should be reminded of the *varieties* of religious experience.

William James took over the distinction which Francis Newman drew between once-born and twice-born characters. He reviewed the religious experience of the healthy minded, the optimistic extroverted psychological type, and then examined the religious experience of the sick soul, the process of unifying the divided self through various forms of conversion. Saintliness and mysticism were next analysed and appraised, and the book ended with the statement of the author's provisional conclusions. He found in the subconscious the point of contact between ourselves and a higher region of being. The conscious person is continuous with a wider self through which saving experience comes. The existence of this mystical or supernatural region seemed to James undeniable, and contact with this higher order of existence has practical effect on character and on the personal centres of energy of various subjects. He rejected the challenge of the scientific rationalist to the validity of any such over-belief.

I can, of course, put myself into the sectarian scientist's attitude and imagine vividly that the world of sensation and of scientific laws and objects may be all. But whenever I do this, I hear that inward monitor of which W. K. Clifford once wrote, whispering the word 'bosh!' Humbug is humbug, even though it bear the scientific name, and the total expression of human experience, as I view it objectively, invincibly urges me beyond the narrow 'scientific bounds'.[1]

From the rationalist and scientific humanist side, the tendency to dismiss all religious experience as illusion is endemic and persistent. William James has to meet the contentions that religious experience is essentially morbid, a perversion of sexual emotion perhaps, and that it is physiologically conditioned and so is nothing but the

[1] William James, *Varieties of Religious Experience*, p. 519.

reflection in consciousness of the state of one's nerves or one's digestion. He had also the positivist dismissal of religious belief as the afterglow of primitive animism, for which positive science had no further use. William James countered these suggestions by pointing out that our science is just as certainly conditioned physiologically as our religion, and we do not on that account dismiss science as illusion. The veridical character of some religious experience he thought might be established by certain criteria. Such experiences are guaranteed by their immediate luminousness, their philosophical reasonableness and moral helpfulness. The last criterion affords the best answer to those who contend that drugs or auto-suggestion could produce the visions and voices which often play a part in outstanding experiences of conversion. No doubt visions attend the consumer of opium and hashish, but such visions have no such lasting and beneficial results as a genuine religious experience. On the contrary, they weaken the character. There may have been a neurotic element in the make-up of Saul of Tarsus, John Bunyan and George Fox, and this may account for some features in the story of the conversion of each. But in all three examples, the man is re-made psychologically, morally and intellectually by his vision. This does not happen to the drug addict.

William James was criticized for concentrating attention on outstanding and even bizarre examples of religious experience. Someone described the book as the yellow-journalism of religion. This was unfair, but it is true that he dealt with clear-cut types and neglected the experience of more ordinary folk. The corrective is supplied in an admirable lecture by C. C. J. Webb, who reminds us that there is a serious danger of overlooking the existence of a genuine religious experience, which although taking forms less strange and striking, is not therefore less real and significant, in a vast number of persons who, though innocent of mystical raptures or of crises of conversion, yet pass their lives against the background of a constant consciousness of being in the presence of a Power behind appearances, a Disposer of events, a Judge of conduct to whom or to which they are responsible and owe reverence, and more or less regularly discharge their debt in ways dictated by the traditions and habits of the social group to which they belong.[1]

Simone Weil has noted the love of religious practices as a kind of implicit love of God. This plays no small part in the religious experience of those whose awareness of God's presence is dim or rudimentary.

William James' reliance on the subconscious as the medium of contact between ourselves and the higher spiritual region, laid his position open to the assessment of the subconscious in the new analytical psychology. Freud found the roots of religion in wishful thinking, and in the influence of childish experience and early teaching. The child needs the protection and authority of his father, and most men remain children all their lives and project the idea of a great spirit on the universe because they cannot get on or feel happy without a Father to protect them and lay down the law for them. In religion and morals, it is said, we perpetuate and re-echo the teachings of father or nurse. Duty is not the stern daughter of the voice of God. It is merely the echo of the voice of parent, nurse, or teacher. So a psychologist of this school can announce: 'Psycho-

[1] C. C. J. Webb, *Religious Experience*, pp. 37–8.

analysis has severed the very roots of religion by showing that it belonged to the unreal and phantasmal, and that it carried all the marks of child-mentality.'

The announcement is premature and indeed betrays the presence of wishful thinking at the heart of rationalism. The rationalist lays himself open to a devastating *tu quoque*.

A reckless young student, who had a smattering of psychology, once attacked William Temple with the accusation: 'You only believe what you believe because of your early upbringing.' The Archbishop promptly dispatched him with the reply: 'You only believe that I believe what I believe because of my early up-bringing, because of your early up-bringing.'[1]

The Harvard psychologist, Professor G. W. Allport, who cites this incident, drives home the similar criticism that must be passed on Freud himself.

If, as Freud says, the religious sentiment is at bottom an extension of one's attitude towards one's physical father, then we must expect repressed animosity towards this father on occasion to be reflected in a hatred of religion. It seems curious that, while Freud insists that belief in God is a projection of dependence and love associated with the earthly father, he overlooks the fact that by the same token atheism may be construed as the projection of ambivalence or hatred associated with the male parent.[2]

A more complete refutation of the attempt to dismiss religion as illusion on the strength of psychoanalysis is to be found in the fact that theologians and pastoral psychologists like the late Fearon Halliday and Oskar Pfister, who

---

[1] *The Individual and his Religion*, p. 122.   [2] *Ibid.* p. 116.

could accept and use Freud's psychoanalytic method, and who would use it only after submitting themselves to deep-going analysis, not only retained, but deepened and strengthened their religious faith and convictions. The testimony of the Oxford psychologist, William Brown, may suffice on this point.

One would expect, according to the Freudian theory, that deep analysis would leave the patient less religious than he was before. My own experience has been the exact opposite. The analysis had indeed a purifying effect upon my religious beliefs, freeing them from much that was merely infantile and supported by sentimental associations or historical accidents. But the ultimate result has been that I have become more convinced than ever that religion is the most important thing in life and that it is essential to mental health; although mere emotionalism and religiosity are diminished, the essentially religious outlook on life remains unimpaired.[1]

It is tolerably clear by this time that Freud's rationalism and atheism have no real support in his psychology. He was in fact, a very poor philosopher, whatever be the final estimate of psychoanalysis. The change of mind to which Professor W. T. Stace of Princeton confesses in his recent book, *Religion and the Modern Mind*, is symptomatic of a growing realization of the weakness of Freud's attempted solution of the dilemma of religious knowledge. He wrote (p. 221):

On the question, is any religion true? I should myself until recently have replied with an unqualified *no*. Religion, I should have said, is nothing but a mass of false ideas and superstitions

[1] W. Brown, *Mind and Personality*, p. 268.

of which the ultimate source is wishful thinking. We have believed in a world that we want to believe in, namely, (one) that is ruled by a power which is friendly to us and to the values of beauty and goodness which we cherish. As a result of further study and reflection I have modified this opinion. To the question asked, I now find the answer to be a qualified *yes*.

So we must, after all, consider what measure of success in the search for truth the poet, and the lover, the mystic, the saint and the prophet may have had. We cannot just dismiss them all as the victims of illusory wishful thinking.

Before I attempt to characterize the contributions of these seekers after truth, I must note an attempt on the part of Dr Julian Huxley to do justice to religious experience as an emotion while discounting it as an avenue to truth, in order to preserve the claim of natural science to a monopoly of the genuine knowledge of objective reality. Julian Huxley repudiates the suggestion that religious experience is something morbid—a neurosis that has the curious advantage of ridding folk of other neuroses! On the contrary, it is a healthy, valuable element in human nature. As he sees it, the only possible solution of the conflict or tension between religion and science is 'for religion to admit the intellectual methods of science to be as valid in theology as everywhere else, while science admits the psychological basis of religion as an ultimate fact'. Huxley accepts Otto's analysis of the sense of the sacred in his book, *The Idea of the Holy*. Otto, I may point out in passing, supplemented William James' definition of religious experience at a vital point. James distinguished religious experience from other forms of experience by an element of solemnity.

Solemnity is a hard thing to define abstractly, but certain of its marks are patent enough. A solemn state of mind is never crude or simple—it seems to contain a certain measure of its opposite in solution. A solemn joy preserves a sort of bitter in its sweetness: a solemn sorrow is one to which we intimately consent.[1]

Otto made clear the nature of this solemn state of mind. He pointed out that certain occasions in life—the birth of a child or the death of a friend, for example—and certain aspects of nature normally evoke the sense of the sacred. We find ourselves in the presence of a *mysterium tremendum et fascinans*—a mystery at once humbling and attractive, awe-inspiring and uplifting. Such experience is an ultimate psychological fact. It is normal and desirable, but it is, according to Julian Huxley, purely emotional and entirely subjective. 'Personal religion, in the form of a disciplined mysticism, a trained reverence aimed at enlarging and harmonizing the microcosm of the individual personality, provides the chief road to certain types of satisfying experience and desirable being.'[2] Huxley denies that mystical experience involves knowledge of, or communion with, a God external to ourselves, but the experience is a good thing in itself, like feeling well, or falling in love. Huxley also recognizes that the religious experience not only humbles and uplifts, but also makes a demand on us for service and dedication. Wordsworth's lines in the *Prelude*, describing his return from a festivity in the early dawn of a new day illustrate the point.

[1] *Varieties of Religious Experience*, p. 48.
[2] Julian Huxley, *Evolutionary Ethics*, p. 56.

Magnificent
The morning rose, in memorable pomp,
Glorious as e'er I had beheld—in front
The sea lay laughing at a distance: near
The solid mountains shone, bright as the clouds
Grain-tinctured, drenched in empyrean light:
And in the meadows and the lower grounds
Was all the sweetness of a common dawn—
Dews, vapours, and the melody of birds,
And labourers going forth to till the fields.
Ah! need I say, dear Friend! that to the brim
My heart was full; I made no vows, but vows
Were then made for me; bond unknown to me
Was given, that I should be, else sinning greatly,
A dedicated Spirit. On I walked
In thankful blessedness, which yet survives.

This feature of the mystic or poetic experience, the scientific humanist can appreciate. As H. G. Wells puts it, 'the desire for service, for subordination, for permanent effect, for an escape from the distressful pettiness and mortality of the individual life, is the underlying element in every religious system'. But the scientific humanist cannot go as far as this unless he is willing to go further. Religion as a state of feeling, whether of mystical exaltation or of dedication, is not desirable in itself, apart from the object which inspires reverence or apart from the nature of the cause to which we give ourselves. To reverence what is not worthy of reverence, or to serve a cause which is not universal or which is mistaken or fictitious, may enlarge and even harmonize the microcosm of individual personality, but it does not provide a road to a satisfying experience, or desirable being. Huxley gives his case away when he assumes that a mystic experience is a good thing in itself, like feeling well, or falling in love. But feeling well when you are not really well is no blessing, and to fall in love with an unworthy man or woman is not an occasion for congratulation. The young man in Dickens' story who fell in love with a hairdresser's dummy was not having a desirable experience. When he gave up his faith in *God the Invisible King*, H. G. Wells still thought he could maintain the attitude of loyalty to him. 'If there is no sympathetic personal leader outside us, there is at least in us the attitude we should adopt towards a sympathetic personal leader.' But without the leader, the attitude becomes irrational, and the attitude will, in practice, be related to unworthy leaders. As an isolated psychological fact or emotional experience, devotion to a leader, or falling in love, is a worthless sentimentalism. We cannot honestly or rationally be religious unless there is someone or something in the Universe it is worth while to be religious about. The value of a religious experience depends, not on the intensity of the experient's feeling, but on the nature of the object which evokes it.

We come back, then, to our main question: What have the poet and lover discovered? What can we learn about the object of religious experience from the mystic, the saint and the prophet? All these seekers after truth are concerned with values, and religion may be defined as the belief in the conservation and cosmic significance of true values. I suppose it is arguable that anyone who values anything has a religion of a kind. The connoisseur in food and drink may have almost a religious feeling about insensitive treatment of the dishes or the wines which he so highly and delicately appreciates. I remember how a contemporary of mine at a high table shocked his seniors by mixing lemonade with his glass of college port, in a spirit of frivolous iconoclasm. It seemed little short of sacrilege to those who knew the bouquet and the date of the port! But it is with higher values that the lover and the poet are usually concerned. For the lover, I might recall Coventry Patmore's poem 'Revelation', or Shakespeare's sonnet,

> Let me not to the marriage of true minds
> Admit impediment: love is not love
> That alters when it alteration finds,
> Or stoops with the remover to remove.

The great challenge, 'Love is not Time's fool' is the direct answer to the philosophy put in the mouth of the dying Hotspur, 'For thought's the slave of life, and life's Time's fool, and Time that takes survey of all the world must have a stop!' 'Love's not Time's fool'—a feeling rather than a reasoned conviction—the manifesto of romantic love which will require something more than romantic love to sustain and justify it. The poet and the lover are obviously kinsfolk, almost identical twins. But the poet has, as part of his calling at least, to make us see the worth and beauty of familiar things, and also to discover worth and beauty in unexpected things. He is to make the desert blossom as the rose. Rupert Brooke's account, in a letter to F. H. Keeling, of his experience as a poet should be known to all Cambridge men.

It consists in just looking at people and things as themselves —neither as useful nor moral nor ugly nor anything else; but just as being. What happens is that I suddenly feel the extra-ordinary value and importance of everybody I meet and almost everything I see. In *things* I am moved in this way especially by some things: but in people by almost all people. That is, when the mood is on me. I roam about places—yesterday I did it even in Birmingham!—and sit in trains and see the essential glory and beauty of all the people I meet. I can watch a dirty middle-aged tradesman in a railway-carriage for hours and love every dirty greasy sulky wrinkle in his weak chin, and every button on his spotted unclean waistcoat. I know their states of mind are bad—but I'm so much occupied with their being there at all, that I don't have time to think about that. I tell you that a Birmingham gouty Tariff Reform fifth-rate business man is splendid and immortal and desirable.... It's a feeling, not a belief, but it's a feeling that has amazing results. I suppose my occupation is being in love with the universe—or (for it's an important difference) with certain spots and moments and points of it.[1]

Rupert Brooke recognized the affinity of his poetic experience with mysticism. Indeed mysticism is the word he uses as the most satisfying label for the mood that comes over him and the attitude to life that results from it. But he refused to translate feeling into belief. He did not embrace any philosophy of mysticism. 'Do not leap or turn pale at the word Mysticism', he writes to Keeling, 'I do not mean any religious thing or any form of belief.' Moreover, he was conscious of a difference—a profound difference—between his approach and the characteristic approach of the mystic. The mystic is concerned with the universe as a whole; with some harmony, some spirit that runs through

[1] *Collected Poems of Rupert Brooke, with a Memoir*, pp. liiif.

all things and binds all things together, but Rupert Brooke is in love, not with the universe so much, as with 'certain spots and moments and points in it'. *The Great Lover* is not the best of his poems, but it faithfully reflects this interest of the poet in particular things and persons. Wordsworth's lines composed a few miles above Tintern Abbey reflect the more characteristic mystical sense of a presence that is in but also beyond all thinking things and all objects of thought. An awareness of a power within and beyond the universe, and a feeling of oneness with this power, stamp the mystic.

Sometime in 1927, Professor C. D. Broad gave an address to the Student Christian Movement in Cambridge on the grounds of faith in a personal God. On another occasion, Professor Broad wrote:

If any reader who is interested in this subject will study Butler's *Analogy*, Hume's *Dialogues on Natural Religion* and the theological parts of Kant's three *Critiques*, he will learn all that the human mind is ever likely to be able to know about the matter, with just one grave omission. The omission is that he will find nothing about the claims of specifically religious and mystical experience to give information about this aspect of reality.[1]

In his address to the Student Christian Movement, Professor Broad surveyed and evaluated these claims.

Finally, I come to the argument for the existence of God which is based on the occurrence of specifically mystical and religious experiences. I am prepared to admit that such experiences occur among people of different races and social traditions, and that they have occurred at all periods of history.

[1] *Five Types of Ethical Theory*, p. 11.

I am prepared to admit that, although the experiences have differed considerably at times, and although the interpretations that have been put on them differ still more, there are probably some characteristics which are common to all of them and which suffice to distinguish them from all other kinds of experience. In view of this, I think it more likely than not, that in religious and mystical experience, men come into contact with some Reality or some aspect of Reality which they do not come into contact with in any other way. But I do not think there is any good reason to suppose that this Reality which manifests itself to certain men in religious and mystical experience is personal. I think that we are inclined to believe this because we are most familiar with the religious experiences of Western Europeans and of Jews, most of whom have put this interpretation upon them. We do not know, or we forget, that the mystics and religious teachers of the Far East on the whole definitely reject this interpretation. And we are inclined to forget that certain Europeans, such as Plotinus and Spinoza, who have had these experiences, also reject this interpretation of them. I think on the whole, then, that there is no inductive argument which makes it at all highly probable that there is a personal God.

Clearly, when he addressed the Student Christian Movement in these terms, Professor Broad agreed in advance with Professor Stace, that the answer to the question, is any religion true? should be a qualified *yes*. He rejected the view that mystical and religious experiences are merely emotional and provide no clue to the nature of Reality. On the contrary, he held it probable that such experiences provide us with knowledge of Reality, or of some aspect of Reality, which cannot be communicated to us in any other way. But the true interpretation of the evidence of such experience remains in doubt, and indeed he suggested that we are faced with two conflicting interpretations, and the evidence as he assessed it does not permit us to choose between them with any confidence.

I cannot help thinking that Professor Broad too readily assumed that the two divergent interpretations of the nature of the reality disclosed in mystical and religious experience are contradictory and mutually exclusive. They may be complementary, and East and West may both be right in what each asserts, and wrong in what each denies. The mystical experiences which lead to such different interpretations need not be identical, though possessing in common characteristics which mark them off from other kinds of experience. The two types of mystics, Eastern and Western, may be in touch with different aspects of the same Reality. We should surely all agree that God is not *merely* personal, or at least that personality in God cannot be fully understood by the nature of personality in ourselves. What God is in himself we cannot know, and, as Dr John Owen says somewhere, our knowledge of God at its best is but a vision of his back parts. The truly reverent believer must be agnostic. But nevertheless he has a positive faith which he holds as rooted or verified in experience. Now the content and the interpretation of our religious experience will vary according as we are preoccupied with God as he may be known to us, or with God as he is beyond the range of our conceiving. There can be no true religion without these two elements; God would not be God if he could be fully known to us, and God would not be God if he could not be known at all. It is not surprising that there should be two types of mysticism according as men's minds are directed towards the one or the other of these truths. But an experience and an interpretation dominated by the first, as we see it in Plotinus, for example, cannot invalidate an experience and an interpretation based on the second. Similarly, as it makes a difference whether the mystic is looking for God outside nature or within it, so it makes an even profounder difference whether God is sought and found beyond history or within it. Both quests may be legitimate. Certainly God cannot be exhaustively revealed in history, in spite of Benedetto Croce, but as certainly, if history has any real meaning or significance, God must be in it, and he will be in it as disposer of events and judge of conduct. Now to the typical Hindu mystic, God lies beyond history; to the true Christian mystic God is gloriously and convincingly present within it. Their interpretation of their experience will naturally differ, but it is idle to appeal to Hindu mysticism as if it negated Christian mysticism.

Dr Adolf Deissmann drew attention to a possible classification of mystics as acting and reacting. The first are the great seekers in search of a Reality that is seemingly passive and awaits discovery. These are the men and women who deliberately choose and tread the mystic way, and prepare themselves for the satisfying experience by the kind of discipline to be found in the Hindu Yoga systems, which Aldous Huxley and Gerald Heard are now commending to us. But there are others to whom mystic experiences come unbidden and unsought. They are reacting to an approach or appeal from the Great Beyond. Let me illustrate it by citing Estlin Carpenter's description of just such an experience. It is recorded in a letter which Dr Bouquet included in his *Lectionary of Christian Prose*. J. Estlin

Carpenter wrote to a friend: 'I was in a condition of religious apathy for a long time when I was at college. I had no intellectual doubts.... But though I had no doubts, I had no religion. I had no sense of personal relationship with God.... ' J. S. Mill, in a similar condition of spiritual apathy, was saved by the nature-mysticism of Wordsworth's poetry. Estlin Carpenter was saved by an actual mystic experience in the course of a summer holiday in North Wales.

I went out one afternoon for a walk alone. I was in the empty, unthinking state in which one saunters along country lanes, simply yielding oneself to the casual sights around which give a town-bred lad with country yearnings such intense delight. Suddenly I became conscious of the presence of someone else. I cannot describe it, but I felt that I had had as direct a perception of the being of God all around me as I have of you when we are together. It was no longer a matter of inference, it was an immediate act of spiritual (or whatever adjective you like to employ) apprehension. It came unsought, absolutely unexpectedly. I remember the wonderful transfiguration of the far-off woods and hills as they seemed to blend in the infinite Being with which I was then brought into relation. This experience did not last long. But it sufficed to change all my feeling. I had not found God because I had never looked for Him. But he had found me; He had, I could not but believe, made Himself personally known to me. I had not gone in search of a satisfying emotion: I did not work myself up into this state by any artificial means. But I felt that God had come to me. I could now not only believe in Him with my mind, but love Him with my heart.[1]

[1] A. C. Bouquet, *A Lectionary of Christian Prose*, p. 196.

This will suffice, I trust, to make clear the distinction between the acting and reacting mystic. The former are the seekers; the latter are the sought, not the finders, but the found. The former are those who have come to know God: the latter are those who discover with St Paul that God has taken note of them. By the former, the great Reality may be interpreted impersonally, though by them, too, even in the East, personal terms are often felt to be inevitable. But to the latter, the great Reality must be personal. And the fact that many of the acting mystics are content sometimes with an impersonal account of the great Reality, leaves the claim of the reacting mystic unaffected. For if you admit that his experience is valid, you must also admit that his experience is as profound as the other's and his understanding of it necessary. That God takes the initiative, that he knows, guides and loves us, that he is touched with the feeling of our infirmities — these are the foundation-verities to which the Christian mystic reacts. This means that God in some real sense must be personal. For love is not a vague or diffused influence, nor is it a principle to be handled with mathematical precision as Mrs Eddy supposed. Love does not exist except in persons. In the full sense, it is a relation between persons. If God be not personal, we might be able to retain Spinoza's intellectual love of the Deity. We could still personify God and so love him. But he could not love us. A strange conclusion and I think an untenable one. Love cannot endure merely as a one-way traffic system. It depends on reciprocity. At any rate, Christianity stands or falls with the conviction that God first loves. Christian experience depends on this conviction. That is why the question of faith in a personal God is so fundamental; that is why an affirmative answer should be enriching, and why a negative answer tends to poverty. It is difficult to see how a philosopher who once admits the validity of the mystic experience, can resist the conclusion that the interpretation of the reality disclosed in it as personal, springs out of the richer experience and contains the deeper truth concerning God:

CHAPTER VI

THE QUESTION OF ETHICS

IN the beginning of the century under review, there was a large measure of agreement as to the nature of moral obligation and as to the standards of conduct by which men were bound. The moral order was held to be as objective as the natural order. Ignorance and defiance of the moral law would be visited with punishment as surely as ignorance and defiance of natural law. If consequences took time to mature, they were nonetheless certain. The mills of God grind slowly, but they grind exceeding small.

Their confidence in the objective character of ethical distinctions and standards became the sheet-anchor of many Victorians when their religious beliefs were shaken or obscured. Indeed, they found their way back to faith through their loyalty to their moral convictions. F. W. Robertson, of Brighton, would say to young men in difficulties with their religious beliefs: 'When a man feels the ice of doubt cracking beneath his feet, one loyalty will bring him through. It is still better to be truthful than to be a liar, to be brave than to be a coward, to be chaste than to be incontinent.' Somewhat in the same vein, Horace Bushnell, when beset by doubt, describes how loyalty to a fundamental ethic led to his recovery of religious convictions. He wrote, that in the crisis when everything he believed seemed to be called in question, he said to himself: 'Is there then no truth that I do believe? Yes, there is one, now that I think of it: there is a distinction of right and wrong that

I never doubted and I see not how I can: I am even quite sure of it.' So long as men retained their faith in the validity of the distinction between right and wrong, it was supposed they would find their way back to God. This is one implication of Tennyson's line about the faith that lives in *honest* doubt. So long as the doubt is honest, i.e. dictated by loyalty to truth, it will bring men to a religious faith. So in the seventeenth century, George Fox taught, 'Mind that which is pure in you to lead you to God'.

For many Victorians, then, the foundations of morality seemed more secure than the foundations of their religious faith, or rather the firmness of the foundations of morality underpinned and helped to secure the structure of their religious faith. Dr Dale at one time endorsed John Stuart Mill's declaration that 'the only view of the connexion between religion and morality which does not annihilate the very idea of the latter, is that which considers the Deity as not making, but recognizing and sanctioning, moral obligations'. 'Moral obligations are not derived from the will of God, but are independent, necessary and eternal.'[1] This seems to suggest that the eternal law of Righteousness exists independently of God, and that God himself is subject to it, even as we are. The confidence of the Victorians in the reign of moral law could hardly be more emphatically expressed.

Dr Dale later modified this view, and realized that the relation of God to the moral law must be differently conceived, if recognition of objective standards in ethics is to lead men to God. 'The law does not claim Him as the most illustrious of its subjects; it is supreme in His supremacy.

[1] A. W. W. Dale, *Life of R. W. Dale*, p. 217.

His relation to the law is not a relation of subjection, but of identity.... In God, the law is *alive*: it reigns on His throne, sways His sceptre, is crowned with His glory.'[1]

It must be remembered that Mill's position, which Dale at one time endorsed, was in no small degree a reaction from Calvinism. In Calvinism the sovereignty of God had sometimes been interpreted as if God were above moral law, beyond good and evil. Standards which are binding on men are not binding on God. We may not judge God's actions by our moral standards. God is just and righteous, but not by any human standards of justice and righteousness. Against this John Stuart Mill protested, and many theologians endorsed his protest. Morality is annihilated if it is derived from the will of God and if the will of God is conceived as arbitrary and even capricious. But if moral obligations are neither derived from nor dependent on the will of God, then the religious sanction for morality may be superfluous and the recognition of moral obligations as necessary and eternal will not recreate faith in God. In any case, men may be moral without religion. Mill and others were quite convinced that essential morality would not suffer through the decay of religious belief. A fundamentally Christian ethic would survive, even if positive Christian convictions decayed.

In the Victorian era, it looked as if this judgement would hold good. Ill-advised Christian apologists who declared morality would collapse if any article of the Apostles' Creed were called in question, were confronted with the spectacle of agnostics and atheists whose moral integrity was beyond question. The case of the good atheist was

[1] *Op. cit.* p. 219.

presented romantically in Edna Lyall's novel *Donovan*, which made a great impression on many in my youth. But much more important was the impression made by such men as J. S. Mill, T. H. Huxley and Leslie Stephen. George Eliot likewise truly interpreted and profoundly influenced the Victorian age, because she retained her faith in morality when she lost her faith in God. It is worth while to recall the reminiscence in which F. W. H. Myers recorded his impression of her attitude of mind.

> I remember how at Cambridge I walked with her once in the Fellows' Garden at Trinity, on an evening in a rainy May, and she, stirred somewhat beyond her wont and taking as her text the trumpet-calls of men—the words, God, Immortality, Duty —pronounced with terrible earnestness, how inconceivable was the *first*, how unbelievable the *second*, and yet how peremptory and absolute the *third*. Never, perhaps, had sterner accents affirmed the sovereignty of impersonal and unrecompensing law. I listened, and night fell: her grave, majestic countenance turned towards me, like a Sibyl's in the gloom: it was as though she withdrew from my grasp, one by one, the two scrolls of promise and left me the third scroll only, awful with inevitable fate.[1]

Myers was to devote his life to the attempt to recover the second scroll, or at least to find empirical evidence of human survival beyond death. But he must have felt George Eliot's commendation of the third scroll to be the more admirable, because she took away the first and second scrolls.

[1] Cited by R. H. Hutton in *Modern Guides of English Thought in Matters of Faith*, p. 271.

Manifestly, the sensational argument of Guy Thorne's *When it was Dark* must be relegated to the scrap-heap, in spite of the commendation of Winnington-Ingram, who was Bishop of London when the novel appeared. The author imagines that some archaeological evidence having been produced to disprove the resurrection, the belief in the resurrection was at once surrendered, and within three weeks, social morality broke down and modern Europe might be described in the terms in which St Paul described the Roman world in the first chapter of his letter to the Romans. No such sudden collapse would have followed any such discovery. A wise seventeenth-century divine, Moses Amyraut, observed that Cicero is a better moralist than theologian. The Roman advocate is much more certain and positive in the description of our mutual obligations in his books *De officiis* than he is in theology in his *De natura deorum*. Amyraut thinks this is typical of Greek and Roman philosophers, and concludes: 'God having purposed that the world should subsist to a certain time has presided in an especial manner over the minds of Legislators and Philosophers to guide them to teach things suitable for the conservation of human society and over the minds of the people in general to cause them to comprehend and to conform to the same.' Certainly there are moral standards in Western civilization which go further back than Christianity and which might survive though the West ceased to be Christian.

The great Victorian tradition is fortunately not dead. There are still among us, or there have recently been among us, philosophers who regard freedom of decision and moral responsibility as psychological facts, and who are not afraid to speak of knowing ethical principles. We have not just got a *feeling* of moral responsibility, we *are* morally responsible and we know it. There is a distinction between right and wrong which we cannot ignore. There are standards we are bound to accept. Thus, Susan Stebbing wrote in *Ideals and Illusions*: 'It is no illusion but uncontested fact that here and now we know that hatred, cruelty, intolerance and indifference to human misery are evil; that love, kindliness, tolerance, forgiveness and truth are good, so unquestionably good that we do not need God or heaven to assure us of their worth' (p. 212). J. S. Mill and George Eliot would have said Amen to that.

The climate of opinion today is very different from that of the Victorians. The kind of knowledge in matters ethical which Susan Stebbing still claimed is widely questioned now. Many who share her moral preferences would doubt the propriety of calling these preferences knowledge. Assessing the present situation, Mary Scrutton of Reading University recently wrote:

There is now a very powerful confluence of ideas—anthropological, psychological and plain logical—undermining our belief in objective morality. In ethics, as in theology, traditional doctrine is opposed by the virtues of the age quite as much as by its vices, and among these virtues is a deep respect for everything that looks like a scientific truth. Logical positivist ethics contends that, as there is no scientific truth in moral subjects, there is no truth at all, only the expression and production of emotions.

At the close of his *History of Western Philosophy*, Bertrand Russell tells us:

There remains a vast field, traditionally included in philosophy, where scientific methods are inadequate. This field includes ultimate questions of value: science alone, for example, cannot prove that it is bad to enjoy the infliction of cruelty. Whatever can be known can be known by means of science: but things which are legitimately matters of feeling lie outside its province (p. 862).

We cannot know that sadism is evil: we can only feel that way. Bertrand Russell hates the infliction of cruelty as much as Susan Stebbing did, but the philosophy of logical analysis forbids him to say, as she said, that he *knows* the infliction of cruelty is bad, unquestionably bad. Strictly speaking he cannot know that any things are *legitimately* matters of feeling, since the same philosophy consigns all such things to the realm of the unknown and unknowable. He had arrived at this position in his book, *Mysticism and Logic* which has recently appeared in a new flight of Pelicans.

Human ethical notions are essentially anthropocentric and involve, when used in metaphysics, an attempt however veiled, to legislate for the universe on the basis of the present desires of men.... To regard ethical notions as a key to the understanding of the world is essentially pre-Copernican. It is to make man, with the hopes and ideals which he happens to have at the present moment, the centre of the universe and the interpreter of its supposed aims and purposes. Ethical metaphysics is fundamentally an attempt, however disguised, to give legislative force to our own wishes (pp. 107 f.).

But, similarly, to claim knowledge in the realm of ethics, to claim objective validity for our moral judgements is merely an attempt to give legislative authority in human society to our own tastes. 'The passions that inspire Nietzsche's philosophy are different from those that inspire the Sermon on the Mount, and those who share one set of passions will agree with the one, while those who share the other will agree with the other.'[1] There is nothing more to be said in the absence of agreed criteria. *De gustibus non disputandum*. It was the advance of this tide of moral scepticism that provoked Dr Waddington to initiate his symposium on *Science and Ethics*, in the hope of discovering some scientific basis for ethics, in spite of the Logical Positivists.

It would take too long to enumerate the many factors that have led to the change in atmosphere. Many strands in modern scientific knowledge—the study of heredity and of endocrinology (i.e. glands), as well as Freud's psycho-analysis—have tended to show that the area of moral responsibility is far more contracted than theologians and Victorian moralists imagined it to be. The elements of priggishness and hypocrisy in the social conventions, particularly in the bourgeois social conventions of the Victorian era, came in for incessant castigation. Lytton Strachey started the fashionable sport of debunking the great Victorians, and along with it went the abandonment of their faith in moral law. In the Edwardian period, Sir Oliver Lodge could declare that the modern man is no longer worrying about his sins—not necessarily that the modern man did not recognize any sins, but the sins he recognized he was confident he could avoid. In 1903, Robertson Nicoll observed: 'In considering the idea of sin,

[1] From a review in *The Nation*, December 1919.

it would, perhaps, be true to say on the whole that the modern mind as expressed in modern literature recognizes clearly only two sins, cruelty and treachery.'[1] The condemnation of cruelty and treachery as evil, if not sinful, is still a feature of our British way of life. We still entertain this preference, though the Logical Positivists hesitate to condemn those who approve cruelty and treachery as legitimate means to desirable ends. But in Europe generally, in an age of world wars and violent revolution, the maintenance of these insights has become precarious. Unfortunately, it is not uncontested fact that here and now we know that hatred, cruelty, intolerance and indifference to human misery are evil. The Fascist and the Communist may regard them as evil and yet the Fascist did and the Communist does deliberately foster hatred, perpetrate cruelty, and act without concern for human misery. Nor can we in the West put on airs of moral superiority when we remember our merciless bombing of civilians and our frivolous use of the atomic bomb. We have let the plea of necessity lead us to condone much that we know to be evil. Our faith in moral progress has been sadly shaken. Between the wars, Delisle Burns hazarded the judgement that no one would now sanction the use of torture for any purpose whatever. This was just before the rise of Hitler to power, on the verge of a period in which torture, physical and psychological, was to be more pitilessly employed on a larger scale than in the time of the Inquisition at its worst. It serves no good purpose to try to measure ourselves against previous generations. It is enough that we are not better than our fathers.

[1] T. H. Darlow, *Life and Letters of W. Robertson Nicoll*, p. 353.

Next to the denial of fundamental moral values in the orgy of cruelty and treachery let loose in the wars, and practised in the totalitarian régimes, the most obvious departure from Christian standards is in the realm of sexual ethics. Robertson Nicoll once wrote: 'I can never sufficiently admire the penetration of Voltaire in singling out chastity as the main point of the ethical teaching of Christianity.'[1] If the nineteenth-century virtue of thrift is now under a cloud, the virtue of chastity is even more heavily discounted. The revolt against the Victorian interpretation of the Christian ethics of sex was not without its justification. Sex was surrounded, in Victorian times, by an atmosphere of hush-hush and prudery which was certainly unhealthy. The repression of sex-interest and the severe condemnation of offenders against sex-ethics have been found to be psychologically unsound and morally dubious. Perhaps I may illustrate this by a criticism directed against the Christian ethic in its Victorian dress. In an article in the Rationalist Press Annual, 1930, Bertrand Russell declared the Church's conception of righteousness to be socially undesirable because it undervalues knowledge and overvalues marital fidelity.

Take, for example, two men, one of whom has stamped out yellow fever throughout some large region in the tropics, but has in the course of his labours had occasional relations with women to whom he was not married: while the other had been lazy and shiftless, begetting a child a year until his wife died of exhaustion, and taking so little care of his children that half of them died of preventable causes, but never indulging in illicit

[1] *Op. cit.* p. 353.

sexual intercourse. Every good Christian must maintain that the second of these is more virtuous than the first. Such an attitude is, of course, superstitious and totally contrary to reason.

We may, I think, concede to Lord Russell, that some, perhaps many, good Christians in the Victorian atmosphere would have adopted such an attitude. But on reflection, it will be clear that the good Christian is under no obligation to judge the second man more virtuous than the first. Indeed, as a good Christian, he ought not to judge men at all, still less to compare them and assess comparatively their merits. All that a good Christian is obliged to maintain is that the good servant of science and humanity would have been a better man if he had not had occasional relations with women to whom he was not married, and that the absolute rotter would have been, if possible, an even more absolute rotter if he had not had the shred of virtue which at least kept him faithful to his wife. While the criticism of Christian morality contained in this particular example misses fire, yet the suspicion that Christians set too high a value on chastity in the scale of virtues remains.

Mr Harrod's chapter on Bloomsbury in his *Life of John Maynard Keynes*, and Keynes' own paper on his early belief, should be read to appreciate the reaction against Victorian Philistinism and the traditional morality associated with it. Positively, under the influence of G. E. Moore's *Principia Ethica*, the group round Keynes and Lytton Strachey found the supreme value of life in states of consciousness involved in human relations and in the appreciation of beauty. Something like absolute frankness and tolerance must mark good human relations, and

'Bloomsbury cordially agreed that the Victorian codes were harsh and brutal and replete with hypocrisy, and that the cobwebs must be swept away'.[1] Keynes says that, at the beginning of the twentieth century he was an immoralist as far as traditional moral codes were concerned, and that he failed to recognize their importance for the social order. Later, in assessing his earlier belief, he made this confession.

We had no respect for traditional wisdom or restraints of custom. We lacked reverence, as [D. H.] Lawrence observed and as Ludwig [Wittgenstein] with justice also used to say—for everything and everyone. It did not occur to us to respect the extraordinary accomplishment of our predecessors in the ordering of life (as it now seems to me to have been) or the elaborate framework which they had devised to protect this order. Plato said in his *Laws* that one of the best of a set of good laws would be a law forbidding any young man to inquire which of them are right or wrong, though an old man remarking any defects in the laws might communicate this observation to a ruler or to an equal in years when no young man was present. That was a dictum in which we should have been unable to discover any point or significance whatever. As cause and consequence of our general state of mind, we completely misunderstood human nature, including our own.[2]

Actually, in the rebound from Victorian stuffiness, we have tended to go to the other extreme. R. F. Harrod suggests that the successors of the original Bloomsbury group still discuss the problems of human relations in a spirit of frankness, but 'what is being said sounds, surely,

[1] R. F. Harrod, *Life of Keynes*, p. 181.
[2] *Two Memoirs*, pp. 99–100.

very crude and callow—so crude and callow that it may call forth a reaction in some more sensitive spirit who might found a society whose main principle shall be that the tender and delicate affairs of the heart shall only be allowed by a strict convention, to be discussed with a sole confidant, and that all this crude gossip and un-feeling comment should be most strictly ostracised'.[1] But, Bloomsbury apart, we think and talk far too much about sex today. We suffer from over-stimulation of sex-emotion—in literature, in the cinema and even in advertisement. Few things have done more to lower the prestige of the West in Eastern lands than the exhibition of films full of sex-appeal. In the West, something like the old Cyrenaic philosophy tends to prevail. Men live for the experience of the moment, too often for the pleasurable experience of the moment. They expect too much from romantic love. As Alfred Marshall said: 'True marriage is not two people living *for* one another, wrapped up in one another, but two people living *with* one another for some worthwhile cause.' The casual associations into which men and women enter so lightly and which they abandon so easily debase the currency in which the heart's affection should be minted. At once overrating and abusing sex-experience, men end in cynicism, and forfeit the happiness that can only be found in the commitment of a lifelong loyalty. We shall not go back to Victorian conventions, but we might well raise our standards of modesty and renew our acceptance of the Christian ideal of marriage.

Speaking more generally, the salvaging of Western civilization and the creation of a world civilization, require

[1] *Op. cit.* p. 183.

the general acceptance of certain values. Schweitzer put first reverence for life, regarding our failure to hold life sacred in all its forms as the primary cause of the decay of our civilization. Important as this is, a deep sense of the sacredness or worth of human personality is even more important, and reverence for life in general has not always guaranteed such respect for humanity. Along with a sense of the worth of the individual person must go a firm belief in the solidarity of the human race, a belief in a kinship which transcends the differences of class, nation and race. We need a conscious recognition that all forms of war, including class-war, are wrong, and all who believe in winning their ends by violence are antiquated reactionaries. We must pin our faith to co-operation and trust, to love and understanding in all human relationships. This requires from us the respect for, and loyalty to truth on which the pursuit of knowledge depends.

If the exponents of the philosophy of logical analysis are right, we must not regard such values or principles as absolute or universal. Indeed, we should frankly recognize that these are personal preferences, the values which we, and possibly the community to which we belong, happen to appreciate and believe in at the moment. Discussing political appraisals in empirical politics, Mr T. D. Weldon lays down some tests, rough and crude tests he calls them, but tests which appeal to me as they do to him, for deciding whether or not Communism is superior to democracy. But he insists that this is his personal view, or prejudice if that word is preferred. It has nothing philosophical about it and may be rejected by anyone who disapproves of it. In his book *States and Morals*, he concludes that 'there can be no universal moral standards without a world State to formulate and maintain them: and no world State can be a State, that is, can govern, unless it enforces the kind of moral theory which its own nature postulates. But in the absence of any demonstration that one political faith is absolutely superior to the others, the idea of a super-State as a voluntary organization is untenable' (p. 286). But Mr Weldon, and those who think with him, believe that, to recognize moral standards as the preferences of persons and societies, will not weaken their influence or diminish our loyalty to them. Indeed, such recognition will have the advantage of delivering us from fanaticism and Pharisaism, and we shall discuss differences in moral standards or judgements with less heat and more profit. While I appreciate the value of a philosophy which allays fanaticism and disarms self-righteousness, I share Dr Waddington's misgivings as to the moral confusion that is likely to result from Logical Positivism in conjunction with other sciences. But in any case, the philosophic position of the Logical Positivist school seems to me unstable, and indeed, in the last analysis, indefensible. As I have already argued, the simple identification of genuine knowledge with natural science and its method is a mistake. 'Whatever can be known, can be known by means of science.' '[The Logical Positivists] confess frankly that the human intellect is unable to find conclusive answers to many questions of profound importance to mankind, but they refuse to believe that there is some "higher" way of knowing by which we can discover truths hidden from science and the intellect.'[1] At the same time they tell us,

[1] Bertrand Russell, *History of Western Philosophy*, pp. 863–4.

THE QUESTION OF ETHICS

'the true philosopher is prepared to examine *all* preconceptions'. Is it not time, then, that as true philosophers,
they examine their own preconceptions? For their refusal
to believe that there is some 'higher' way of knowing by
which we can discover truths hidden from science and the
intellect, is nothing but an unanalysed preconception. If
the human intellect cannot find *conclusive* answers to many
questions of importance, including the questions, what
ought we to do? and what ought we to be?—it does not
follow that we have nothing to guide us but our own desires
and preferences. There is, after all, much empirical evidence
to be found in history which cannot be assessed by the
methods of natural science. There is such a thing as our
common humanity, desires common to us all, the desire to
remain alive, the desire for health and happiness, and there
are common rules of prudence and moral obligations
arising therefrom. Nor can we halt there. There are desires
which may be latent in many, but which nevertheless
ought to be universal. When Bertrand Russell says:
'Morally, a philosopher who uses his professional com-
petence for anything except a disinterested search for
truth is guilty of a kind of treachery',[1] what does he mean
by 'morally'? Does he mean that such a philosopher is
acting in a way he personally dislikes, offending Earl
Russell's taste, rejecting Earl Russell's personal views or
prejudices? Does he mean merely that such a philosopher is
failing to reverence some idol of the whole tribe of philosophers, breaking the rules of the game? The language
'guilty of a kind of treachery' seems a bit rhetorical for
anything so trivial. In fact, the disinterested search for

[1] *Op. cit.* p. 863.

truth is a moral obligation resting on all of us. Earl Russell has stumbled on something like a moral absolute and feels constrained passionately to affirm it.

I cannot myself see that our relation to the moral order, and our understanding of it, differ fundamentally from our relation to the natural order and our understanding of it. The search for truth in science is inspired by emotions and desires just as much as the search for goodness in morality. The distinction between right and wrong, good and evil, is just as objective as the distinction between truth and falsehood. Indeed, the distinction between truth and falsehood is a special case of the more general distinction between right and wrong. There is no science without morality—objective morality. The obligation to choose the good and eschew the evil is just as absolute as the obligation to prefer truth to a lie. We need to be disciplined and disinterested in the search for the good as in the search for the true. Our conception of what is good and right may be as fallible, as liable to error and as much in need of revision as our scientific conceptions and theories, but progress in understanding is as possible and may be as real in morality as in science. It is as irrational to describe our moral standards as merely personal or social preferences as it would be to say that our scientific theories are merely what we like to believe to be true at the moment. As to the suggestion that seems to emerge from Mr Weldon's view of the relation of States and Morals, that States formulate and maintain moral codes and are apparently final arbiters, so that what the State ordains is right for that State and its citizens, this kind of ethical relativism is quite indefensible. I think Professor Stace adequately exposes the fallacy when he offers a strictly parallel argument in the realm of science.

We believe that the earth is globular, but there was an age and culture in which it was believed that the earth is flat, therefore the earth is globular now in our culture, but it was flat in that age and in that culture.[1]

Group relativism is the view that what pleases a society is good within that society and for that society, but not outside it. Translated into practice, what this means is that what Germany likes is morally right for Germany, and what Russia likes is morally right for Russia. This is political relativism, i.e. ethical relativism in politics, and it is equivalent to a total absence of morality as between nations, and this is exactly what we see in practice.[2]

In this situation, the philosophy of logical analysis brings no relief. In fact, it aggravates it.

We cannot but admire those who, like Susan Stebbing, hold fast to objective moral standards and are so sure of their ground that they do not need God or heaven to support them in their moral convictions. It is of course necessary to distinguish morality and religion, and we cannot equate them or make either simply subservient to the other. But there is an intimate connexion between them, and if we have good reason to believe in God and heaven, such belief would strengthen our sense of moral obligation and affect our understanding of our moral code. The recognition of a spiritual order, in which both the natural order and the moral order are involved, would enable us to

[1] W. T. Stace, *Religion and the Modern Mind*, p. 118.
[2] *Ibid*. p. 121.

appreciate the true significance of both science and morality. A passage from Dr Dale will drive home the point I am trying to make.

The spiritual universe is no more to be made out of a man's head than the material or the moral universe. *There*, too, the conditions of human life are fixed. *There*, too, we have to respect the facts: and whether we respect them or not, the facts remain. *There*, too, we have to confess the authority of the actual laws: and whether we confess it or not, we shall suffer for breaking them. To suppose that in relation to the spiritual universe it is safe or right to believe what we think it pleasant to believe—to suppose that because we think it is eminently desirable that the spiritual universe should be ordered in a particular way, therefore we are at liberty to act as though this were certainly the way in which it is ordered, and that though we happen to be wrong, it will make no difference—is preposterous. . . . No belief of ours will change the facts or reverse the laws of the spiritual universe. It is our first business to discover the laws and to learn how the facts stand.

The concluding chapter will deal with the quest for the Jesus of history and the return to the Christ of faith. The quest was undertaken largely in the hope of discovering in the historic Jesus a supreme moral lawgiver. It has ended in the discovery that he is moral law-giver only because he is much more. His significance in the moral order derives from and depends on his significance as revealer of the spiritual order.

CHAPTER VII

THE QUEST FOR THE JESUS OF HISTORY AND THE RETURN TO THE CHRIST OF FAITH

A<small>T</small> the outset of his massive work *Christ in Modern Theology*, which was published in 1893, Dr Fairbairn noted a striking contrast between the theological library of 1850 and the theological library of his own day.

What was *not* found in the library of 1850 would be to us more remarkable than what was, especially its poverty in books dealing with Jesus as an historical person. Books of a kind would indeed be here abundant. Harmonies of the Gospels, bearing great names... and exhibiting extraordinary feats of conciliatory exegesis: defence of miracles, and especially the Resurrection, against deists and deniers of every sort: poetic presentations of sacred history... edifying and devotional works... but hardly a book attempting to conceive and represent Him just as He appeared in history would have been found (p. 17).

The historical approach to the New Testament as a whole and to the Gospels in particular supplied this defect. Dr Fairbairn was well aware that the process of inquiry was not completed, but he thought the recovery of the historical Christ had gone so far that towards the close of the nineteenth century, we could claim to know 'Him as no other age had done, as He lived and as He lives in history, a Being who looked before and after, within the limits and under the conditions of time and space, influenced by what preceded Him, determining what followed'.[1] The Christian theologian can now stand and must now stand 'face to face with the historical Christ and conceive God as He conceived Him. What God signified to Jesus Christ, He ought to signify to all Christian churches.' Fairbairn regarded this as a kind of Copernican revolution in theology. In previous creative and revolutionary changes in Christian thought, more often than not the most potent influence had been Pauline.

Paul [wrote Fairbairn] has been at all times what he was in his own—the greatest of all the Apostolic forces that work for evolution and change. But the modern return is to Christ, and to Him as the Person who created alike the Evangelists and the Apostles by whom He is described and interpreted. He has become the centre from and through which all are studied, and is not simply looked at through the eyes of Paul or John.[2]

I cannot attempt here to trace the steps by which men recovered the knowledge of the Jesus of history, but I must note one or two landmarks in this development in this country during the latter half of the nineteenth century. The publication of Strauss's *Life of Jesus*, in an English version by George Eliot, created a great sensation but exerted no lasting influence in this country. It gave a fillip to rationalism, and 'soon, in England, working people who had never heard the name of Strauss or the title of his book, were repeating the rumour that a German scholar had proved Christianity a fraud'.[3] By exaggerating the possibilities of myth in the gospel-traditions, Strauss opened

[1] Dr Fairbairn *op. cit.* pp. 20 f.   [2] *Ibid.* p. 187.
[3] C. C. McCown, *The Search for the Real Jesus*, p. 5.

the door to the Christ-myth theorists, but his book was so ponderous, so negative and so obviously dominated by Hegel's philosophy that it failed to capture the support of historical scholars or the interest of educated readers. George Eliot was thoroughly bored by it, and only her strong sense of duty made her complete it. As Professor C. C. McCown observes, Strauss together with the Christ-myth school from Bruno Bauer to Arthur Drews, and indeed together with the tendentious criticism of Ferdinand C. Baur of Tübingen, belongs to a false start in critical inquiry, led by philosophy instead of historical science.

The writer who really captured the interest and imagination of the intelligentsia of England was Renan, whose *Vie de Jésus* appeared in 1863. The nature of Renan's undertaking is clearly indicated in a searching review by Dean Church:

M. Renan's process is in the main the reverse of Strauss's. [Strauss resolving the content of the Gospels into myth.] Renan undertakes to extract the real history recorded in the Gospels; and not only so, but to make it even more palpable and interesting, if not more wonderful, than it seems at first sight in the original records, by removing the crust of mistake and exaggeration which has concealed the true character of what the narrative records: by rewriting it according to those canons of what is probable and intelligible in human life and capacity which are recognised in the public whom he addresses.

The first of these canons is 'the assumption that in no part of the history of man is the supernatural to be admitted'.[1] A second canon will be one of psychological probability. Renan will interpret events and persons in terms of what he

[1] *Occasional Papers*, vol. II, p. 193.

thinks morally and psychologically probable. His life of Jesus was the first of many attempts to understand and describe the origins of Christianity 'according to the normal canons of human history, without prejudice and without miracle'.[1]

Renan's successors are the radical French critics, Loisy and Guignebert. Loisy closed his volume on *The Birth of the Christian Religion* with the confident assertion: 'In the whole course of this remarkable evolution nothing happened which cannot be explained by the laws that govern human life' (p. 358). Guignebert's position is essentially the same. Both French critics eliminate the supernatural and both rely on their estimates of what is psychologically probable. Both appeal, like Renan, to the laws, psychological and sociological, that govern human history, though in the understanding of these laws they differ from Renan and from one another.

Renan's book had an immense vogue. Its appeal was something like the appeal of the Bellman's map to his crew in *The Hunting of the Snark*. In contrast with the other maps, the Bellman's perfect and absolute blank was a map they could all understand. Renan's portrait of Jesus was far from being an absolute blank. It was full of colour, but it was a portrait all could understand. Here was a Jesus of history who was not mysterious, but credible to the educated and half-educated reader who accepted Renan's canons of what is probable in human life. The *Vie de Jésus* was taken for gospel in many quarters.

Renan distinguished and contrasted two periods in the

[1] Gilbert Murray, Preface to Loisy, *The Birth of the Christian Religion*, English Translation, p. 5.

ministry of Jesus. In the first, Jesus appears as a simple peasant with profound intuitions into the secret of noble living, full of sweetness and light, presenting his gospel of love naïvely and hopefully to Galileans who do not really understand. In the second period, perceiving that his message will only win its way if backed by authority and miracle, he claims to be Messiah and he claims to work miracles, though he knows as we know that miracles do not happen. The raising of Lazarus Renan took to be a deliberate deception, a trick to impress a credulous public. The first period is sunny and optimistic, the second is cloudy and stormy and ends in frustration and failure. F.D. Maurice summarized Renan's view in a letter in this way: 'M. Renan's Jesus is a charming Galilean with a certain sympathy for beautiful scenery and an affectionate tenderness for the peasants who follow him: but he is provoked to violence, impatience, base trickery as soon as he finds his mission as a reformer unsuccessful.'[1] Similarly Dean Church wrote of Renan:

His view is that a Galilean peasant, in advance of his neighbours and countrymen only in the purity and singleness of purpose with which he realized the highest moral truths of Jewish religious wisdom, first charming a few simple provincials by the freshness and native beauty of his lessons, was then led on, partly by holy zeal against falsehood and wickedness, partly by enthusiastic delusions as to his own mission and office, to attack the institutions of Judaism, and perished in the conflict—and this was the cause why Christianity and Christendom came to be and exist.[2]

[1] *Life of F. D. Maurice*, vol. II, p. 462.
[2] Church, *Occasional Papers*, vol. II, p. 195.

The manifest defect, not to say absurdity, of Renan's view lies in his combining a belief in the moral supremacy and integrity of Jesus with the belief that he claimed supernatural powers which he knew to be delusions and bolstered up the claim by trickery and deception. Few today would entertain Renan's conception of moral likelihood. Another defect lies in the preponderance of sweetness over light in Renan's narrative. There is too much sugar in it for modern taste and historic truth: it is too romantic and too sentimental. Nevertheless readers of the *Vie de Jésus* were given a vivid picture of the Galilean background and an indelible impression of the charm of the first proclamation of the good news by Jesus. Luke tells us that in the synagogue at Nazareth, the hearers were astonished at the gracious words which fell from Jesus' lips. Some chapters of Renan's book are an extended commentary on this text. The *Vie de Jésus* had a legitimate appeal.

The influence of Renan also persists in the acceptance of the idea of two contrasting periods in the ministry of Jesus, although the contrast is interpreted somewhat differently and Renan's preposterous suggestion about the raising of Lazarus is eliminated. Obviously, if we follow Mark's narrative, Peter's confession of Jesus as the Christ at Caesarea Philippi marks a decisive turning-point in the story. Baron von Hügel in one of his essays noted and defined the contrast almost in Renan's terms:

Thus, as before Caesarea Philippi, the kingdom was conceived prophetically as a relatively slow and peaceful growth, and from Caesarea Philippi onwards, it was conceived apocalyptically—as a sudden violent irruption: so also before Cassarea, the Messiah appears most lowly, radiant and with all-embracing hope, and from Caesarea Philippi onwards, as coming again in the clouds of heaven with power.[1]

Middleton Murry's life of Jesus provides a somewhat similar variation on Renan's theme.

In 1865, Macmillan published a work by an anonymous author entitled *Ecce Homo*, which eclipsed the fame and interest of Renan, at least for English readers. Six editions were issued before the end of 1866, and the seventh edition which appeared in 1867 was reprinted no less than fifteen times before 1893. The author was the historian, J. R. Seeley, and it was some time before his name was revealed, though Sidgwick knew him to be the author before he wrote a review in June 1866. Seeley proposed to give a survey of the life and work of Jesus Christ from the historical side and to refrain from discussing theological issues. He was trying, as he said, to furnish an answer to the question: 'What was Christ's object in founding the society which is called by his name, and how is it adapted to attain that object?' But the very fact that Seeley made no avowal of his faith and kept silence about doctrines, aroused suspicion. It was supposed that he must be an unbeliever, and good Earl Shaftesbury declared that such a dangerous work must have been vomited from the mouth of hell. However, as Charles Morgan says, in his *History of the House of Macmillan*, Gladstone fortunately disagreed with the Earl. Gladstone wrote to Alexander Macmillan who had sent him an advance copy:

I will not draw out the long catalogue of its praises: but I will venture to say that I know of, or recollect, no production of

[1] Baron von Hügel, *Essays and Addresses on the Philosophy of Religion*, 1st ser. p. 123.

equal force that recent years can boast of, and that it is with infinite relief as well as pleasure that, in the present day, I hail the entrance into the world of a strong constructive book on the Christian system.[1]

Henry Sidgwick was almost as appreciative: 'I have had the work of Christ put before me by a powerful hand and been made to recognize its extraordinary excellence as I have never before done.'[2] His review was less favourable, written when he thought *Ecce Homo* would turn out a broken reed. Dean Church devoted to the book a long, discriminating and appreciative article which commended it to the attention of thoughtful readers. It is some tribute to the character of the book that during the time the secret of its authorship was undisclosed, it was conjectured to be from the pen of writers so eminent and yet so different as J. S. Mill and J. H. Newman!

Seeley not only eschewed theological issues, he also passed over many historical problems, since he did not write a life of Jesus like Renan's, but was content to bring out the essential features of Christ's ministry and teaching. The book is in two parts. In the first, he presents Christ as the King of the coming kingdom. The baptism is the call to Messiahship. The temptations are the temptations of the Messiah: how is he to fulfil his calling? He is conscious of possessing supernatural power: how is he to use it? The authority with which he speaks is regal. He calls his disciples to form a new society, a commonwealth through which God's will shall be done on earth. In the second and

[1] D. C. Lathbury, *Letters on Church and Religion of W. E. Gladstone*, vol. II, p. 88.
[2] A. and A. M. Sidgwick, *Henry Sidgwick, A Memoir*, p. 145.

longer part, Seeley presents the teaching as Christ's legislation for the society he came to found. This approach no doubt appealed to Gladstone, both as statesman and churchman, for in a sense Seeley conceived the mission of Jesus in the categories of political science.

Ecce Homo is at once a more virile and a more reverent book than Renan's *Vie de Jésus*. Seeley penetrated more deeply into the mind and purpose of the Jesus of history. He is free from Renan's sentimentalism and from his condescending patronage of a Jesus as a peasant *illuminé*! Critical readers questioned Seeley's use of the Gospel sources and at a later stage, he was thought to have identified the kingdom of God too closely and too simply with the Church. But it is difficult to overestimate the service he rendered to his contemporaries and can still render to us today. As Dean Church said: 'Most of us read the Gospels with sealed and unwondering eyes.' Alas! it is still true. For his generation, Seeley opened men's eyes to the wonder of the central figure of the Gospel-story. So Dean Church concluded:

Here we leave this remarkable book. It seems to us one of those which permanently influence opinion, not so much by argument as such, as by opening larger views of the familiar and the long-debated, by deepening the ordinary channels of feeling and by bringing men back to seriousness and rekindling their admiration, their awe, their love, about what they know best.[1]

It is not strange that men were moved by *Ecce Homo*. It would have been strange if they had not been.

[1] *Occasional Papers*, vol. II, p. 178.

In his original preface, Seeley declared his intention of preparing another volume which should deal with Christ as the creator of modern theology and religion. This sequel never appeared and indeed Seeley was not qualified to produce it. He was a historian, not a theologian. As I have already indicated, the task which Seeley saw to be necessary and failed to execute, Fairbairn undertook at a time when such a reading of the character, purpose and message of Jesus as Seeley offered seemed satisfying and convincing. The literary critics had by this time established the priority of Mark's gospel, and Seeley had taken Mark as his fundamental authority. The earliest gospel, it was supposed, consisted of trustworthy historical reminiscence, little, if at all, distorted by tendential bias or theological interpretation. The record of the teaching of Jesus common to Matthew and Luke, was held likewise to rest on the bedrock of history. So Fairbairn could claim that his generation knew Jesus better than previous generations. Some such clear account of Jesus' message concerning the Fatherhood of God and the worth of the human soul as was presented in Harnack's remarkable book, *What is Christianity?* seemed to do justice to the essentials of the Gospel.

Harnack's book, the last manifesto of the Liberal school, appeared in 1900, and very shortly afterwards, Fairbairn's confidence in our knowledge of the historical Christ, based on the critical study of the Gospels and represented to us in such books as Harnack's *What is Christianity?* and Seeley's *Ecce Homo* was profoundly shaken, if not shattered, by two new developments in the study of Christian origins. First, Alfred Loisy and Albert Schweitzer insisted that the clue to the mission and message of Jesus must be found in eschatology, in the expectation of the coming of the kingdom of God in the near future in the form of some dramatic catastrophic divine intervention in history. The coming of the kingdom, not the Fatherhood of God, was the essential message of Jesus. We pass over this feature of the gospel-record because it means little to us, but it meant everything to Jesus and the first disciples. In the second place, the Form-critics appeared on the scene, declaring that there is little or no simple historical reminiscence in the Gospels. Incidents and sayings were remembered, selected and embellished in the interests of the life and propaganda of the Church. We have to ask of each item in the record, what is its place in the life of the Church, or rather in the life of the young nascent Christian communities both Jewish and Hellenist? Approached in this way, we must expect to find more interpretation than history in the Gospels. All four Gospels have the same aim as the Fourth. They are written to persuade us to believe in Jesus as the Son of God. It is difficult, if not impossible, to disentangle what Jesus actually said and did from what the evangelists and the churches for which they wrote believed he must have said and done. So Dr R. H. Lightfoot concluded his Bampton lectures with an echo from the Book of Job which many found disconcerting. 'It seems, then, that the form of the earthly, no less than the heavenly Christ is for the most part hidden from us. For all the inestimable value of the Gospels, they yield us little more than a whisper of his voice; we trace in them but the outskirts of his ways.'[1] Fairbairn was premature in supposing that 'Christ had now become the centre from and through which all the

[1] R. H. Lightfoot, *History and Interpretation in the Gospels*, p. 225.

Apostles are studied and is now not simply looked at through the eyes of Paul or John'. When we read Mark we may be looking at Christ through the eyes of Paul, or through the eyes of Peter whose vision may be no clearer or better than Paul's. Some divines hastened to endorse these two new developments as undermining Liberal Protestantism, if not positively favouring a Catholic and orthodox understanding of Jesus. Father Tyrrell, for example, followed Loisy in seeing a possible Catholic apologetic in the thorough-going eschatology of Schweitzer.

The true successors of Seeley, T. R. Glover and J. Middleton Murry, refused to surrender either to thoroughgoing eschatology or to the Form-critics' despair of disentangling the Jesus of history from the Christ of faith. Like Seeley, Glover and Middleton Murry were laymen. Glover was a classical historian, Middleton Murry is a distinguished literary critic. All three made use of the historical imagination and all three had an intuitive insight into something original and central in the message of Jesus. Glover's *Jesus of History*, published in 1917, was to my generation what Seeley's *Ecce Homo* had been to our fathers. Middleton Murry's *Life of Jesus*, or *Jesus Man of Genius* (to use the title of the American edition), which appeared in 1926, was a study in the same genre. I wish I had time to characterize both books in some detail. They are both neglected now, but I believe, with Professor Donald Baillie, that there will have to be a return to these interpretations, more particularly to Glover's *Jesus of History*. Its values are by no means exhausted, nor have its insights been fully absorbed and appreciated. And Glover and Middleton Murry were right in refusing to be stampeded by the eschatologists. Both writers, however, seemed to the main body of critical students of the Gospels a little superficial and even fanciful in their handling of their sources, a little impatient with the detailed study of the synoptic problem. Glover wrote too soon to take account of Bultmann's *History of the Synoptic Tradition,* and I doubt whether Middleton Murry has even heard of it. We had to wait till the Second World War for W. Manson's careful and adequate assessment of Bultmann's sceptical form-criticism in his book, *Jesus the Messiah.* I venture to think that recent studies have justified the hesitation of Glover and Middleton Murry with regard to both the new developments.

Schweitzer has recently written a new preface for a reprint of his famous book, *The Quest of the Historical Jesus.* He stills holds to his thoroughgoing eschatology and insists that Matthew and Mark together point to the acceptance by Jesus of a Jewish apocalyptic scheme of the coming of the Kingdom, to be ushered in by a period of tribulation, as the clue to his conduct and teaching. But he no longer regards the ethic of Jesus as an interim ethic, i.e. as proposing lines of conduct that would only be justified by the conviction that the Kingdom is at hand, and that the time that must elapse before its final consummation will be short. The ethic of Jesus has other sanctions and possesses a timeless eternal validity. This is how Schweitzer states his position today.

The Gospel of the Kingdom came into the world in its late-Jewish form which it could not retain. The Kingdom, expected to come immediately in supernatural fashion, fails to appear and so does the Son of Man who was to arrive on the clouds of heaven. The situation thus created compelled believers to take a more and more spiritual view of the Kingdom of God and the Messiahship of Jesus, the former becoming a spiritual and ethical ideal to be realized in this world, and Jesus the spiritual Messiah who laid its foundation through his ethical teaching. So obvious did this appear that it was taken to be the view of Jesus himself, and his preaching was understood in this sense. All this involves overlooking the words of the first two Gospels which create a different impression.

Respect for historical truth, however, compels our faith to give up this *naïveté* and to admit that it has been subject to development. It can do this without being untrue to itself or to Jesus. It has become what it is under the pressure of a higher necessity, under the influence of the spirit of Jesus.

It was Jesus who began to spiritualize the idea of the Kingdom of God and the Messiah. He introduced into the late-Jewish conception of the Kingdom, his strong ethical emphasis on love, making this and the consistent practice of it, the indispensable condition of entrance. By so doing he charged the late-Jewish idea of the Kingdom of God with ethical forces, which transformed it into the spiritual and ethical reality with which we are familiar. Since the faith clung firmly to the ethical note, so dominant in the teaching of Jesus, it was able to reconcile and identify the two, neglecting those utterances in which Jesus voices the older eschatology.

I may quote a further paragraph which is even more significant:

Jesus is already the spiritual Messiah, as opposed to the Messiah of late-Jewish eschatology, in that he has the Messianic consciousness while living a human life in this world, and feels himself called to awaken in men the desire for the spiritual qualification for entrance into the kingdom. Late-Jewish eschatology only sees the Messiah as the supernatural Lord of the supernatural Kingdom of God. It has no idea of his first appearing on earth as a servant in human form. This came to birth in the consciousness of Jesus. As the spiritual Lord of the spiritual Kingdom of God on earth, he is the Lord who will rule in our hearts.[1]

Even now, it seems to me that Dr Schweitzer does not realize how profoundly this modifies his original contention. He first claimed that the idea of the coming of the Kingdom was conceived by Jesus in terms of late-Jewish apocalyptic and indeed that this late-Jewish apocalyptic literature and tradition were the source of the central conviction which governed and permeated Christ's life and teaching. But it now appears that what we perhaps mistakenly call Christ's ethic, his ethical emphasis on love and on the consistent practice of it, and also his distinctive Messianic consciousness, are not derived from late-Jewish apocalyptic at all. It is open to us to question Schweitzer's first assumption. Since two out of the three fundamental convictions which determine all that Jesus began to do and to say have not their source in late-Jewish eschatology, it is unlikely that Jesus' conception of the coming of the Kingdom coincided with current Jewish conceptions even if some sayings echo the language of Enoch. I would venture to suggest that the confident hope of Jesus as to the coming of the Kingdom had no literary source but was bound up with his unique communion with God which made the Kingdom a personal reality for him. Indeed, the goal of human history and the

[1] A. Schweitzer, *The Quest of the Historical Jesus*, pp. xv–xvi (3rd ed.).

way to it are for him so certain and so clear, that the end seems to be already within reach.

It is not quite enough to say, as Schweitzer says, that Jesus felt himself called to awaken in men the desire for the spiritual qualifications for entrance into the Kingdom. He felt himself called to bring men into the Kingdom, to bestow on them, as it were, in advance, the blessings of the Kingdom, healing of mind and body and the forgiveness of sins. He bade men love their enemies not as a qualification for entering the Kingdom when it comes, but as a way of living as God's children here and now and of doing God's will on earth as it is done in Heaven. His friendship with publicans and sinners was a form of realized eschatology. Jesus was even more concerned with the nature of the Kingdom and its present realization than he was with its future coming and ultimate triumph.

If recent research modifies the thoroughgoing eschatology of Schweitzer and Loisy, it also supplies some corrective of the Form-critics' assumption that we cannot discern the figure of the historic Jesus through the mists of even primitive tradition. In this connexion, I judge that the work of C. H. Dodd and Joachim Jeremias of Göttingen on the parables constitutes a new and important development in the critical study of the Gospels. They demonstrate the truth of Matthew Arnold's dictum that Jesus was above the heads of his reporters. They show that in the tradition of our Lord's teaching by parables, the Evangelists preserved more than they understood, or rather that we can see clearly that this or that parable is original because its situation in the ministry of Jesus is different from its situation in the life of the Church. What we call the parable of the prodigal son is a case in point. In the life and preaching of the Church it becomes the parable of the prodigal son. In the life and teaching of Jesus it was the parable of the elder brother. Jeremias makes the point effectively when he says:

The parables which have as their theme the gospel, are, apparently without exception, addressed not to the poor but to Christ's opponents. That is their special character, their place in life. They are not primarily the offer of the gospel but the defence, the justification of the gospel, weapons in the conflict with the critics and enemies of the gospel.[1]

Of the parable in Luke xv, Jeremias rightly adds:

Without question this parable is addressed to men who resemble the elder brother; the approach is to their conscience. Jesus says to them 'God is so merciful! Be not so loveless! Join in and rejoice.' Again it is clear, the parable is not primarily the presentation of the gospel to the poor, but the defence of the gospel. It is more: it is remonstrance, it sounds the warning note and then breaks off. Jesus' hearers are in the position of the elder brother who must decide whether to give way to the appealing words of his father and join in the festivities or not. Jesus is not threatening or denouncing the Pharisees. He still has hope. This defence of the gospel is meant to woo and win the hearts of his critics.[2]

This one example may suggest the possible outcome of the new epoch in the interpretation of the parables. If we can discern original meanings and applications of which

---

[1] J. Jeremias, *The Parables of Jesus*, p. 100.
[2] *Ibid.* p. 105 f.

those who recorded the parables were unaware, or only half-aware, we may get back to the very words of Jesus and reach a better understanding of his message.

'God is so merciful. He gives sinners and Tax-gatherers a share in his Kingdom though they have not deserved it. God is like that, as kind as that. And because God is like that, I, too, am like that, says Jesus.'[1] This revelation of God in the Jesus of history makes him the Christ of faith. The quest for the Jesus of history set out under the sign, *Ecce Homo*. It was to discover the man, and it expected to find a teacher of ethics, the best and wisest perhaps, but still a teacher pointing us to a truth independent of his person. But when we meet the Jesus of history we find that he is more than a teacher. His mission is, if possible, more important than his message, and his message cannot be divorced from his mission. He shows us what men ought to be and may be, because he shows us what God is. A friend of mine once wrote: 'So much modern teaching about Jesus leaves me without a sure joyous sense of contact with God through him. It sees him merely as a wise teacher, talking beautifully about God, when he is not supposed to be preaching pacifism or social reform. The modernist talks as if we had only *ideas* about God, not God disclosed, not God present with men, not God self-given to men.' But in the Gospels it is precisely the sure, joyous sense of contact with God through Jesus which my friend desired, that is constantly in evidence. It was not for nothing that Matthew claimed for Jesus the title Emmanuel, God present with us.

In his *Adventures of Ideas*, Whitehead says that towards

[1] *Ibid.* p. 10.

the end of his life, Plato reached and published his final conviction,

that the divine element in the world is to be conceived as a persuasive agency and not as a coercive agency. This doctrine should be looked upon as one of the greatest intellectual discoveries in the history of religion.... This is matched by the supreme moment in religious history, according to the Christian religion. The essence of Christianity is the appeal to the life of Christ as a revelation of the nature of God and of his agency in the world.... Can there be any doubt that the power of Christianity lies in its revelation in *act* of that which Plato divined in theory?[1]

The fundamental Christian conviction is, then, that Jesus Christ has come to us from God's side. There is a passage in *The Forsyte Saga* which suggests what the recognition of Christ's divine mission may mean to us today. Jolyon Forsyte, the artist, is digging in his garden with his son who has volunteered for service in the Boer War and is about to sail for South Africa. In a pause in their labours, the son says to his father:

'Do you believe in God, Dad? I have never known.'
At so searching a question from one to whom it was impossible to make a light reply, Jolyon stood for a moment, feeling his back tired by the digging.
'What do you mean by God?' he said. 'There are two irreconcilable ideas of God. There is the Unknowable Creative Principle—one believes in That. And there's the Sum of Altruism in Man—naturally one believes in That.'
'I see. That leaves Christ out, doesn't it?'

[1] A. N. Whitehead, *Adventures of Ideas* (Pelican ed.) pp. 196-7.

Jolyon stared. Christ the link between those two ideas! Out of the mouth of babes! Here was orthodoxy scientifically explained at last! The sublime poem of the Christ-life was man's attempt to join those two irreconcilable ideas of God. And since the sum of human altruism was as much a part of the Unknowable Creative Principle as anything else in Nature and the Universe, a worse link might have been chosen. Funny how one went through life without seeing it that way![1]

This is fiction, but I venture to think, illuminating fiction. Let me buttress it with a confession of faith from a schoolmaster, Mr Vicars Bell. He finds himself believing in a God whose nature is to him a riddle, but, when he turns to Man, he says:

I cannot evade the unasking, inescapable figure of Christ. Nor can I ignore his unspoken claim to be the most perfect expression possible of the inscrutable mind of God. I do not see in his life an explanation of the contradictions of the divine nature, but I see in him a way of accepting these contradictions.[2]

It is indeed not enough to think of the Christ-life as a sublime poem, as man's attempt to link two irreconcilable conceptions of God. The Christ is no myth, no embodiment of wishful thinking, nor yet a lay-figure decked out in garments woven by devout imagination. Try as we may, we cannot get him out of history, and if we have any sense of reality, we cannot evade his challenge. He thought he was sent, sent from God, to fulfil God's promise to his people; sent from God to be a light to lighten the Gentiles.

[1] John Galsworthy, *The Forsyte Saga*, p. 604.
[2] Vicars Bell, *The Dodo*, p. 169.

He believed his death was needed to establish God's rule among men, to make clear the majesty of God's mercy. Christ may have been mistaken, but was he? He may have died for nothing, but did he? It is for us to decide. Christ will not force our judgement. He takes his Kingdom with entreaty, and keeps it with lowliness of mind. He seeks the unforced devotion of loyal hearts. And those who love and follow Christ will know the living and true God.

BIBLIOGRAPHY

ALLPORT, Prof. G. W. *The Individual and his Religion.* Constable, 1951.

BELL, VICARS. *The Dodo.* Faber, 1950.

BOUQUET, A. C. *A Lectionary of Christian Prose.* Longmans, 1940.

BROAD, C. D. *Five Types of Ethical Theory.* Kegan Paul, 1930.

BROOKE, RUPERT. *Collected Poems, with A Memoir.* Sidgwick and Jackson, 1926.

BROWN, W. *Mind and Personality.* University of London, 1926.

BUSHNELL, H. *Nature and the Supernatural.* Lowe, 1861.

CHURCH, R. W. *Occasional Papers*, 2 vols. Macmillan, 1897.

DALE, A. W. W. *Life of R. W. Dale*, Hodder and Stoughton, 1898.

DARLOW, T. H. *Life and Letters of W. Robertson Nicoll.* Hodder and Stoughton, 1925.

FAIRBAIRN, A. M. *Christ in Modern Theology.* Hodder and Stoughton, 1893.

FORSTER, E. M. *G. Lowes Dickinson.* Arnold, 1934.

FREUD, S. *Future of an Illusion.* Hogarth Press, 1928.

GALSWORTHY, J. *The Forsyte Saga.* Heinemann, 1922.

HARROD, R. F. *Life of J. M. Keynes.* Macmillan, 1951.

HOOKER, RICHARD. *Laws of Ecclesiastical Polity.* Dent, 1907.

HORT, A. F. *Life and Letters of Fenton J. A. Hort.* Macmillan, 1896.

HÜGEL, BARON VON. *Essays and Addresses on the Philosophy of Religion.* J. W. Dent, 1921.

HUTTON, R. H. *Contemporary Thought and Thinkers.* Macmillan, 1894.

HUTTON, R. H. *Modern Guides of English Thought in Matters of Faith.* Macmillan, 1900.

HUTTON, R. H. *Aspects of Religious and Scientific Thought*. Macmillan, 1899.

HUXLEY, JULIAN. *Evolutionary Ethics*. O.U.P., 1943.

INGE, DEAN. *The End of an Age*. Putnam, 1948.

JAMES, WILLIAM. *Varieties of Religious Experience*. Longmans, 1902.

JEREMIAS, J. *The Parables of Jesus*. S.C.M. 1954.

JOWETT, B. *Essays and Reviews*. Parker, 1860 (2nd ed.).

KEYNES, J. M. *Two Memoirs*. Hart-Davis, 1949.

LATHBURY, D. G. *Letters on Church and Religion by W. E. Gladstone*. Murray, 1910.

LIGHTFOOT, R. H. *History and Interpretation in the Gospels*. Hodder and Stoughton, 1935.

LOISY, A. *The Birth of the Christian Religion*. Allen and Unwin, 1948.

LOWES DICKINSON. *Religion, a Criticism and a Forecast*. Allen and Unwin, 1920.

LUCAS, F. L. *Journal Under the Terror*. Cassell, 1938.

MAURICE, FREDERICK. *The Life of F. D. Maurice*. Macmillan, 1884.

McCOWN, C. C. *The Search for the Real Jesus*, Scribners, 1940.

NEVINSON, H. W. *Changes and Chances*. Nisbet, 1923.

NEVINSON, H. W. *Visions and Memories*. O.U.P., 1945.

NEWMAN, J. H. *Essay on the Development of Christian Doctrine*. Toovey, 1845.

POLLOCK, J. P. *A Cambridge Movement*. John Murray, 1954.

POWYS, LLEWELLYN. *The Pathetic Fallacy*. Longmans, 1930.

PROTHERO and BRADLEY. *Life and Correspondence of A. P. Stanley*. Murray, 1893.

ROWNTREE, B. S. and G. R. LAVERS. *English Life and Leisure*. Longmans, 1951.

RUSSELL, BERTRAND. *Mysticism and Logic*. Pelican Books, 1953.

RUSSELL, BERTRAND. *History of Western Philosophy*. Allen and Unwin, 1946.

RUSSELL, BERTRAND. *The Scientific Outlook*. Allen and Unwin, 1931.

BIBLIOGRAPHY

SCHWEITZER, A. *The Quest of the Historical Jesus.* A. C. Black, 1954 (3rd ed.).

SIDGWICK, A. and A. M. *Henry Sidgwick, A Memoir.* Macmillan, 1906.

STACE, W. T. *Religion and the Modern Mind.* Longmans, 1952.

STEPHEN, SIR JAMES. *Essays in Ecclesiastical Biography.* Longmans, 1860.

TWEEDSMUIR, LADY. *The Lilac and the Rose.* Duckworth, 1952.

WALTON, R. D. *The Gathered Community.* Carey Press, 1946.

WEBB, C. C. J. *Religious Experience.* O.U.P., 1946.

WHITEHEAD, A. N. *Adventures of Ideas.* C.U.P., 1933.